The Sequence for the Predominance of the Energy Body

Author: Marco Baston
Intent Publishing
Cover illustration: Simone Savina

ISBN: 9791221321401

www.nagualism.org

Marco Baston

THE SEQUENCE

(For the Predominance of the Energy Body)

Intent Publishing

CONTENTS

INTRODUCTION

The Sequence emanates from the blue worlds.

The lineage of men of knowledge I belong to has developed, throughout generations of warriors, a series of movements that allows to attain the predominance of the energy body, if performed by following the right flow in the time mode.

The sequence comes from the direct contemplation of the rule, which is, in essence, the totality of the eagle's commands. For centuries have warriors applied themselves to understanding these energetic dictates. They did it from a protected position, not directly exposed to the eagle.

As far as the sequence is concerned, it refers to that part of the rule that pertains to the human being, and especially to the domains connected to the warriors' activities.

The sequence is the physical and perceptual transposition of the raids the seers that were made (and are still made) into the strategic vision of the unknown. Therefore, it also becomes an actual map, not that different from those left in the stones and structures of pre-Columbian cities.

The map generated by the sequence, however, radiates directly from our bodies: it is always with us.

Since the rule is infinite, so is potentially the sequence; in fact, it is continuously expanded and updated. Variations with very precise and specific purposes can depart from every single movement.

Moreover, the details open worlds of perception that are always different.

It is the task of every generation of warriors to give its contribution to this continuing evolution.

Yet, there is a central core of movements that sums up the fundamental commands, and precisely the ones that allow to obtain the predominance of the energy body.

It is a long and elaborate series, whose purpose is to connect the different arts of a warrior.

These movements are not only physical.

The correct execution is obtained only when we make the body movements correspond to a progression of controlled, predetermined, and strategically disciplined assemblage point shifts that, once learned, are induced according to a precise order and time. These small shifts of the assemblage point produce, at the end, the detachment of the assemblage point from its habitual area and, thus, a new position, preordained by the practice's intent, that favors the memory of the dreamer or, in other words, of the energy body.

Actually, the best way to learn the sequence would be learning the right assemblage point movements in the correct order and time, and only after that, making them coincide with the proper sensations that inevitably produce those same movements.

This is the way my teachers transmitted the sequence to me, which I will describe more in detail below.

I underline this point to highlight an aspect that is basic in the execution of the sequence: if one finds the right sensations, these will determine the correct movements, and not the other way around. This means that it is the sensations that act as guide; if you will not move in the corresponding way, you will neither find nor maintain the correct sensation, that is, the one that causes the strategic assemblage point movement. On the other hand, if you keep the correct sensations, you will necessarily move and position yourself in extremely precise forms, in which every detail determines deep variations in your sensation.

The sequence reproduces the warrior's way step by step, exactly like a map. Indeed, it begins creating a connection with the earth and with the world as emanations at large.

So, during the execution, the apprentices register in their body what will be the various phases of their warrior's path as they enjoy this alliance with the world. In this way, they establish a privileged bond with the earth and can confide in its help when they must make fundamental choices.

Indeed, we cannot do everything alone; it is necessary to have sufficient humbleness to confide in this alliance with infinity, in the connection between the energy body and intent.

The sequence for the predominance of the energy body is, like the recapitulation, a discipline in itself; an activity that, in any case, produces very potent effects on our existence, even if it is not inserted into the warrior's way.

So, the practice of it brings advantageous and effectual changes, even in persons who have not decided to finally adhere to the warrior's world.

This effect is due, just like for the recapitulation, to the fact that, by executing it properly, one inevitably connects with the intent established by generations of seers and to the parts of the rule to which the sequence refers; especially to the ones relevant to the impulse to freedom.

At the end of a good execution of the sequence, we tend to move toward an assemblage point position that warriors call “the place of effectiveness” or “of no self-pity” or “of no pity.” This position is opposed to the ordinary one, which is defined as “place of apprehension.”

If maintained, it gives access to silent knowledge; a condition in which language and linear thinking are excluded, and we become pure action and direct knowledge, operating in synchrony with intent.

It is the condition that causes the real predominance of the energy body.

After the execution of the sequence, like after the recapitulation, one is not the same person anymore (and this is also the sign that we are doing it well).

Both cause deep changes in the configuration of the energy fibers.

There are no other ways of doing it with the necessary harmony; and, without these changes, there is no evolution.

The sequence reconfigures our alignment every time we execute it. So, we have the possibility of starting different directions, of changing, choosing, evolving.

The sequence is also a form of reiteration. That is why it is called “sequence.”

The sequence brings fractions of inorganic energy of a selected type, which is in harmony with our natural evolution process. That is why it gives us vigor and resilience, helps our dreaming, stalking, and connection with intent.

It is a kind of "free" organic energy, disengaged from agreements. It comes from their abstract part that aims, it too, at freedom.

In the course of time, the seers realized that, in order to proceed into the unknown, it is essential to have fractions of inorganic energy at their disposal. The case of dreaming is the most indicative in this respect, but the question concerns everything we do as soon as we exit the domain of ordinariness.

The absence of quotas of different energy is, among other things, also one of the reasons why we humans tend to remain tied to the restricted space we know and fear everything that lies, even just a little, outside the uniformity and repetitive continuity of ordinariness.

The problem for warriors has always been how to obtain this energetic availability without incurring into drawbacks. The solution has actually been always at hand: there is an aspect of inorganic energy that is impersonal and abstract, not connected to the individual will of inorganic beings. This aspect attracts and gathers also those among them who also, like us, long for freedom, the same way in which the essence of the amber energy can guide human beings to emancipation.

The abstract side of the inorganic energy is not particularly connected with the emanations at large of the blue alignments. We do not know the reason for it, but it is so.

The sequence has been obtained by connecting with these alignments, extracting their flow, and thus obtaining a few drops of the purest essence.

SOME PRELIMINARY INDICATIONS

Before I start illustrating the sequence in detail, I want to mention some basic indications, principles, ways of approaching it that one has to be constantly aware of throughout the duration of the sequence, as well as suggestions for its correct execution.

1 – Gathering attention before beginning.

Ideally, the sequence should be preceded with a gazing session, so as to favor the onset of inner silence. Any type of gazing is good, if it is easy for you and quickly establishes a state of silence and intensity. Better yet if it is done as you stand already in the position in which you are going to do the sequence and gaze at the area on which you will have your eyes. While standing like this, bring your attention to the body and the earth, remain aware of this relationship (body – earth) and how the connections are formed that "pull us down," inside the earth. If you do these things well (that is, with attention), you will seize precisely the moment in which to go down to latch onto the earth's lines and start the sequence.

The right way to seize the connections that pull us toward the inside of the earth is to regulate the lateral flows, inserting the hands and maneuvering them delicately and with extreme concentration, until a current is released that hooks onto us, pulling us down.

There is a time, a velocity, of the earth that we have to follow as we go down, in order to remain connected. It will never be the same; every time it is different and decides what will be, that time, the rhythm of the execution of the sequence.

2 – There is no predetermined execution speed.

It changes, as I was saying: from person to person and from time to time. It can also change while doing it. The speed with which you see it done in the video is not a point of reference. The video just shows the movements.

There is a speed suited to each moment in which we execute the sequence, based on the following principle: not being too fast, to avoid letting the effects of the movements reach us and accumulate; but not waiting too long between one movement and the next, to avoid dispersing what has been put together, to prevent the inner dialogue from engaging again, and to remain one with the internal continuity flows.

Control and abandonment. Forbearance and timing.

In principle, it is however better to be slower rather than too fast, at least at a learning stage. The purpose is to be in the body's time and maintain the perception of the flows in the area of possibilities.

3 – You have to be always shifted on your body.

The correct execution of the movements is very important, but it is only a small part and is only in function of the ability to evoke the right sensations.

Indeed, what really counts is this: evoking the right sensations.

Let us start with a basic premise: the world is a sensation; we are a sensation. Handling the world and ourselves as sensations, until this sensation is made real, means to intend.

It is what we continuously do: turning the perception of energy into precise sensations and then work them out and sustain them until they are turned into a concrete reality.

The sequence follows the inverse course.

The sequence bases its power, its extraordinary effectiveness, on the ability to evoke a strategic series of sensations. These sensations correspond to small shifts of the assemblage point, connected and organized with a specific purpose: to cause the predominance of the energy body. All the rest is just trimmings. Therefore, being in the body from the start is basic.

It is the body that knows the right sensations. They cannot be thought.

The description of the sequence, for every movement, indicates beside the explanation of the movement itself the correct sensation to be looked for.

4 – All the movements must be perceived.

Our real mind is the body.

Starting from this fact and adding it to what I said before about the world as a sensation, it becomes clear that the body is our means to transform the physical movements into something much broader and more complex. In synthesis, every movement, even the slightest, has a correspondence, is transferred through physical sensations, into the so-called "area of possibilities." The latter is the condition that allows to handle the area that surrounds and includes the physical body, in short, the luminous egg, the series of layers of energy fibers whose center is condensed into the physical body.

We can control this area directly through the correspondence between physical movements, sensations, and intent. This correspondence turns our movements into something abstract that acts directly on our energy fibers; but in order to do it, we have to be in the will's time.

I dealt with the area of possibilities in the other books and also in some videos; so, to experience it, I refer you to those.

Here I just want to underline what I just said, to avoid misunderstandings: the area of possibilities is the state that allows to acquire control over the energy fibers that make us up, that is, over ourselves.

5 – The Sequence reproduces the different phases of a warrior's way.

The different parts of the Sequence are ordered in such a way as to form a guide for warriors.

First, they establish a privileged relationship with the earth; then, thanks to the latter, they activate the vibratory center and can bring this new control to the will, while they realign their energy fibers correctly, extending them toward the world instead of toward themselves…and so on. The different phases follow each other until the unification with the energy body is reached.

In this way, warriors act according to an order that is not mental but gets activated thanks to the physical understanding of one's possibilities.

In essence, it is sufficient to allow the assemblage point positions induced in series by the sequence to carry out their effect, to settle into the body.

It is another reason why it must be carried out in inner silence; the more silent we are, the more easily we achieve the physical learning.

6 – Maintaining the connection with the earth and the perception of the energy flows.

At the beginning of the sequence, we obtain the connection with the earth; this has to be maintained throughout the whole execution. It is the first fundamental sensation that accompanies us; in fact, it accompanies warriors throughout the course of their existence.

It consists in remembering that we float, we are suspended, in the earth's energy fibers, which are aware, full of intent and devoid of any syntax.

The other fundamental sensation, the perception of the energy flows, surfaces as a consequence of the movements stimulated in our energy fibers by our intending while we perform the sequence.

The fibers literally hook onto our moving body's awareness and follow our shifts. This happens if we intend the right sensations, which act as mediators that trigger and maintain the perception of the continuity between the movements and the area of possibilities.

This continuity pulls and relocates the energy fibers.

It is the sensation of moving within a special density, of having intensity lines and areas located along the spaces through which we move. After a certain time and through practice, these lines and areas start becoming really visible. It is a special seeing that involves a warrior's body in its entirety: it is seeing as the Toltecs mean it.

7 – The use of the eyes.

The use of the eyes is of paramount importance. You will find many details in the part that explains the sequence precisely; however, there are some things that cannot be truly transmitted easily. The best reference you can find, for now, is the section about gazing in the book *The Energy Threshold*.

Aside from this, I will try all the same to provide some basic indications.

First of all, it is necessary to keep a certain mobility of the eyes, that is, to avoid remaining completely fixated. The gazing area, as described below, is precisely an area in which the eyes maintain their mobility. It is a very light mobility, barely hinted at, but it must have two fundamental traits: continuity and softness.

Using the eyes with continuity means that we do not skip from one point to another, as we do in our ordinary way of looking.

We move our eyes without skipping, without a break; the eyes must break loose from the ordinary mind, connect to the will, and be directed by the latter.

Having softness means that our eyes stop judging the world, and this allows the real world to enter, filling us up with the silence that permeates the world itself.

In time and with practice, you will realize that the correct way of using the eyes evokes every single movement's specific intent, permitting the change of the states of attention that take place during the sequence.

From that moment on, the eyes will move following a correspondence with the flows in which the movements are inserted.

8 – Awareness of the position.

As has already been highlighted, physical awareness is essential. This means that we must always be aware of the precise body position; that is, of how we place ourselves exactly in space.

Keep in mind that there are variants in which the sequence is done in total darkness; so, it is not possible to look at ourselves to establish where and how we hold our hands, arms, legs, etc. Furthermore, also in the normal execution are the eyes concentrated on the act of gazing in all of its variants and must absolutely not concern themselves with our position. So, the latter must be exact, precise, correct only through the permanent awareness of our body.

Every gesture, every position based on such awareness must be precise, never neglected. The importance of this is essential, and this precision can only come from developing an accurate sensitivity to ourselves as perceivers and as a group of energy fibers.

I mean that the use of our attention is what counts most: we are made of attention.

During the course of the sequence the attention is gathered, directed, shifted, expanded on parts of the body, on areas that are external to the physical structure, and on the changes in the state of perception. All of this causes the movements of the assemblage point toward very precise positions that correspond to changes in the state of perception and awareness, which lead to the predominance of the energy body.

9 – Coordinating stalking and intent, control and abandonment.

The sequence yields its effects at its highest potential if it is performed in the right state; this right state is nothing but the state of a warrior, a precise harmony between control and abandonment. Control and abandonment are exerted at the same moment, not at separate times; and this is what determines their harmony.

To achieve it, it is essential to coordinate stalking and intent, which is one of the sequence's main objectives. Therefore, as one proceeds in the sequence, enters deeper into it, the progress of their mastery enhances the coordination between stalking and intent, determining the concurrence of control and abandonment. In turn, this makes the sequence become even more effective.

The initial secret is not to have personal expectations, but to coincide with intent.

10 – Favoring the release of the knowledge stored in the legs.

For the whole duration of the sequence, the legs participate actively; they are not inactive appendices on which we simply rest. First of all, they must, from the start, establish a very strong, continuous, and intentional grounding in the earth. It must be really like sinking into the earth and push, causing a return wave. There must be physical engagement.

The density of the earth which we gather at the beginning continues running through us, coming up through our legs.

From this response by the earth we obtain the continuous passage of impulses that intertwine with the fibers of our legs, back, entire body and stimulate them from below, generating micro-movements, like a light current going through our whole body. We are never truly still.

Furthermore, every time we move or readjust our position during the course of the sequence we have to do it by getting the whole body involved through our legs.

11 – Maintaining physical abstraction.

Most part of the sequence is carried out without touching the body, without physical contact (except when it is specified). The purpose is preventing the sensations we are looking for from being associated to ordinariness; and also succeeding in shifting into the area of possibilities and staying in it.

The principle is that the world is a sensation and can be manipulated. Therefore, learn to consider your body, too, as a sensation; to perceive it, first of all, through your "feeling."

12 – Fine-tuning every single movement.

This is a practical advice.

Since every movement has a specific intent and must evoke precise sensations, the advice is to take the passages one at a time to try and search, until the correct sensations are reached; until the specific intent is released.

Proceeding in this way allows us also to develop the necessary patience and discipline, integrating them in the execution of the sequence.

13 – The sequence teaches intending, it corresponds to the ability to intend.

The sequence develops our relationship with intent and the energy body.

It must be approached with this premise, with this awareness that must be kept firmly in mind. Recall it from the start.

Evoking the right sensations is a school, a training-ground for the ability to intend. The effect of the way in which the sequence forges warriors extends then to every aspect of their activities, of their existence.

14 – Storing silence.

Silence leads the movements of the sequence. It hooks and drags them into the empty spaces, into the free spaces in the area of possibilities.

The necessary state requires silence. We look for it from the start, but we store it and maintain it movement after movement. In this way, silence accumulates, exactly as it happens in a warrior's way.

15 – Adjusting the back throughout the whole execution.

Like the legs, also the back participates actively. It is the area in the body that is most open to perception, where fundamental centers are found that activate unbending intent and the control of perception. While we move, and between one movement and another, we must pay attention to the adjustments and to the micro-movements that concern the back, relax it, open it, and connect it to the rest of the body with harmony and continuity.

In many passages, the spine corrects its alignment spontaneously if we let it. The most important moments in which this happens are indicated in the description of the execution.

16 – Position of feet (parallel) and legs.
The sensation will be quite different.

Stay aware of having a firm and well-ordered position of feet and legs. Everything starts from here. The legs are slightly flexed (except for a few passages, where they are straight), we must feel like “sitting,” the muscles are active, never yielding or flabby.

17 – In the sequence, the movements are hooked to the double perception.

Perception does not mean looking.

During the execution of the sequence, we maintain the use of double perception.

I mentioned it in the book on the recapitulation, but I believe it is very useful to resume and go deeper into it, if possible. I say “if possible,” because it is not easy at all to describe it in words; it is a great deal easier to make one experience it directly (and that is what I do in practical workshops).

In any case, having access to double perception translates into the ability to maintain at the same time the ordinary awareness (actually, a much more precise awareness than we ordinarily have) and that of the energy flows. I want to emphasisze two details of what I just said.

Maintain at the same time: therefore, not shifting continuously from one to the other, but being able to sustain them at the same time; intertwined, superimposed, intimately merged; like a single perception and yet clearly separate.

And then, keeping the ordinary awareness and that of the energy flows: I did not talk about seeing, not even feeling. It is true that, in practice, initially we pass through feeling. Later on, however, we free ourselves of this way of defining perception, too.

An exercise to favor double perception.

You can do it while walking or moving in any other way (but actually, once we have overcome the phase of physically understanding the state we have to reach, we can also do it as we stand still), therefore it can be applied in a great deal of situations.

Look ahead and gaze at the area in front of you. Clearly, you must use all of the gazing techniques: soft and continuous gaze, active peripheral perception, etc.

While walking, “hook” onto the elements of the world as you pass them by and do not leave them even when they are past the point where you can see them in the area of your peripheral vision and are finally left behind you.

Continue to perceive and hold them with your body. Initially it is a sort of expanded, tactile gazing and it is difficult to hold. I suggest you start with one or just a few elements at a time.

The double perception becomes operational when a kind of “tug” or release, a separation, occurs. At that point, they flow together: first and second attention.

In this way, the second part of the perception is always kept in the area of possibilities during the execution and is under the control of the will; in the broadest sense, thus, in the area of possibilities of the world, of the world’s elements.

If you can, of the earth. That is why the sequence begins with the earth.

Emanations inside on the full spaces, pure attention on the empty spaces. Tonal and nagual. Connection with the emanations at large.

18 – The movements have continuity.

They are never interrupted, never split. Indeed, we are never still.

There are "internal continuity flows" that connect all the movements. Even when there seem to be phases in which we keep still for a certain time, in reality, a certain level of mobility is always present.

It cannot be perceived from without, by an onlooker; but in time, it becomes very evident to those who execute the sequence. And it is one of the aspects that are fundamental for the sequence to fully express its potential.

We are like water. There are currents and flows, generated by the intent of the movements, which we have to second, with respect to which we have to be yielding. This type of controlled acquiescence is the same that is necessary in order to relate with intent: if we acquire it in the body through the sequence, it becomes a natural part of us.

CENTERS OF POWER AND PERCEPTION

There are parts of the body, areas, zones, that are directly related to our magical possibilities (in other words, to the relationship between attention and energy) and that do not only concern the physical body, but the totality of ourselves.

I will try to offer a particular vision of these centers and of what they really do.

Let us start always from this point of view: the world and we are a sensation.

Some parts of the body have the power to put together and govern the right sensations, those that lead us to intend our magical possibilities (to use our attention in precise and deliberate forms in order to govern definite aspects of energy).

The area of the glow

Physically, it corresponds to the nape of the neck.

It is called like this because, when perceived energetically, the unblocking of this point appears as the release of a glow of heightened awareness.

Obtaining the continuity that results from this unblocking allows to unleash indescribable aspects of energy tied to the nagual and the energy body; aspects of great importance specifically in our relationship with the dreamer (energy body) and with intent.

In practice, intending this continuity, governing the attention on the flow between our back and neck that, starting from the area of the unbending intent, reaches the tip of our skull, is key to governing our nagual.

The center for decisions

The center for decisions governs the quality and intensity of our choices. Better yet: it determines the fact that we make a more or less voluntary, deliberate, free choice. It is directly connected to the area of unbending intent and, therefore, through it, to the will in a triangular connection that, when active, generates a perfect guide for the movements and the positions of the assemblage point.

When we really choose to decide something or even to change something in us, this is clearly and physically very perceivable in this center that corresponds to, or better, is organized in the hollow at the base of the throat. The moment the choice passes through us something similar to swallowing takes place, or a sense of freshness, or a small snap that releases a fraction of unintelligible matter.

The vibratory center

The vibratory center governs the vibratory aspect of energy, the power that literally holds living beings together.

The emanations that make up every being endowed with awareness would have a natural tendency to return to the dark sea of awareness, irresistibly attracted, departing from each other and thus determining the death of the being to whom they belong.

This does not occur as long as one is alive thanks to a very special aspect of energy, the vibratory aspect, which, instead, generates an attractive, agglomerating force that consolidates and compresses the totality of the energy fibers: the true vital force.

It is an aspect of energy that can only be governed by awareness, by beings endowed with attention; and, in fact, it allows living beings to affect the way time functions.

Naturally, the more this aspect of energy is active, the more we are resilient, endowed with clear direction, intense.

Thus, the vibratory center governs the direction of our existence, generates the correct discipline, connects us to the other aware beings, gathers inner strength, and drives back the suggester. Obviously, all of this happens if we are able to consciously activate it.

Physically, it is located approximately at the tip of the sternum, immediately above or below it. Therefore, its effects are confused with the heart; that is why we talk about the "path with a heart."

The vibratory center governs this aspect of energy that, however, is uniformly spread throughout the luminous egg and "envelops" all our energy fibers, every single emanation that makes us up.

If it gets really activated, its effect spreads like magma in our whole being, also because it is strictly related to the option of the fire from within.

In fact, the fire from within occurs the moment the assemblage point coincides with the core of the vibratory aspect, lighting it and connecting all the emanations and all the possible time modes at the same time.

The will

The will is the center par excellence, because it governs the second attention; and therefore, if one cannot discipline it, it is practically impossible to get control over the non-ordinary assemblage point positions, including the ones related to stalking.

Indeed, every assemblage point position that is not the known, ordinary one needs the intervention by the will; as stalkers, in fact, warriors can move to the area of the will even while they are in their daily life.

This gives them a much more effective position from the energetic viewpoint; when they get to this point, warriors do not live exactly in the same way as their fellow men, but in another, a great deal more interesting and richer one. The area of the will keeps them in a time mode that is called "the stalker's dream." It is what allows them to harmonize the principles of stalking and controlled folly in a natural manner.

The area of the will is in the zone around the navel, and the warrior connects to the world from it. It is our real channel for aware connection to the world and to the active side of infinity.

The four intensification points

There are four main points in our body for the intensification of attention.

They can be used both in the waking state and in dreaming to obtain immediately greater clarity and the enhancement of inner silence, or to gather dreaming attention.

Two of these points are in the upper part of the body, under the collarbones, between the collar bone and the shoulder, where there is a little depression: the subclavicular indentation.

These points, for example, can be pressed while gazing to help us stop the inner dialogue or to give us an additional boost into silence.

They are strictly related to inner silence.

The other two are in the sartorious muscle, at the level of the hip joint. When these points are pressed during the sequence, the muscle must always be tense; therefore, we have to keep our knees slightly bent. In this way, it is also easier to find the exact point.

If you press this point in dreaming, your dream becomes at once easier to hold, intensifies, and the dreaming attention remains compact.

Right side

The right side is related to dreaming; clearly, to dreaming as the Toltecs understand it. As a practical application, stimulating the right side correctly facilitates the development and continuance of dreaming in all of its forms, that is, in everything that is related to the possibility to stop the assemblage point at will in the second attention.

In the sequence, much of the work done on the right side has the purpose of bringing a higher level of control within the second attention, so as to obtain uniformity and coherence.

Left side

The left side is related to seeing, in the Toltec meaning of the word. The maneuvers executed on the left side are needed to obtain stability, clarity, and understanding within the states of heightened awareness. They are also aimed at the purpose of guiding us directly toward silent knowledge, without undergoing deviations.

Stimulating the left side correctly makes the energetic vision understandable.

The potential of the left side gathers the ability to understand in inner silence, it makes silent knowledge work, and sublimates the need for syntax.

Moreover, the opening of the left side tends to favor the shift of the assemblage point inwardly, in the direction of the vibratory center. This is a kind of shift that is very advisable for its implications concerning impeccability, that is, the adequate use of the available energy.

The area of unbending intent

This area concerns approximately the lower back. It is linked to the will by a connection that goes through the body. This allows the will to act in tune directly with the unbending intent.

Being able to apply unbending intent means to be capable of maintaining the position or the direction of the assemblage point indefinitely and at will.

Without unbending intent, we would never be able to keep silence or the prerogatives of non-ordinary positions. Moreover, we would have no clarity about the direction to be maintained.

The wings of perception

The upper part of our back, the area around and inside the shoulder blades governs our perceptual capacity and the capacity to intensify it without limits.

From a practical point of view, the more we can spread out, unfold, make elastic, and extend toward the world the fibers that concern this area, the more our perception will be subjected to changes, meaning that, similarly, it will become more expanded.

The sensation is really that of a series of fibers that are entangled and extend outwards, spreading out perfectly outstretched and uniting in an infinitely expanded dimension.

When we really manipulate this area, our perception is immediately modified. The first impressions are of greater lucidity, clarity of vision, depth, or even strange perceptual alterations; always, however, very clear.

The wings of perception are in direct relationship with the vibratory center through fibers that, as a matter of fact, go through our body.

Memory areas

Our legs store fundamental memories and information.

The question, for warriors, is how to free all of this knowledge, making it accessible. The way we use our attention throughout existence ends up getting this information "stuck," becoming stagnant for the rest of our lives.

If we could free it, we would have incredible evolutionary opportunities at our disposal.

These opportunities would also concern the memories of our energy body; indeed, freeing the energy body's memories is the main purpose aimed at by those parts of the sequence that involve the legs. Other goals are to stimulate special points in the legs endowed with the capacity to intensify awareness and awaken the general potential of our inferior limbs' fibers. For this purpose, it is important to continuously get the whole body involved in the actions of the sequence.

Fundamental nodes are the knees and calves; we could say that from there many locks can be picked that open the way to this action for the liberation of knowledge.

The four areas in the diagonals of the peripheral vision

We are accustomed to using our perception in a very limited way. To begin with, we limit ourselves to the visual perception and, normally, we focus our attention on a window in front of us, disregarding almost completely, for instance, our peripheral vision. Thus, the latter remains a mysterious area for us, although very interesting things are found there, from the seers' point of view.

There are four very important areas: two are related to the vibratory center and are up to the right and left, in the area at the limit of our peripheral vision when we extend our arms.

The other two, on the other hand, are perceptually connected to the will and are located, still at the limit of our peripheral vision, down to the right and left.

The four areas draw two diagonals that can produce extraordinary relationships between attention and energy, besides very interesting modifications to the energy configuration.

Moreover, these areas can be used to stimulate the will and vibratory center in various ways. This can be done not only as it is done in the sequence, but also by using, for instance, the movement of natural elements like running water, leaves moved by the wind, fire, and more. The movement is directly transmitted as a sensation into the perception centers and stimulates them in a very interesting way.

In order to use the four zones of the peripheral vision correctly, we have to apply the double perception, and thus unite the peripheral vision to the perceptual sensation that issues from these areas.

The lateral flows

The lateral flows are the organization of two couples of bundles of emanations inside, two front and two hind, arranged vertically. The two front bundles are positioned in front of us at a distance of about 20 – 40 cm from the body, facing the intensification points. This distance can actually vary according to our state: it depends on the exact connections made by the flows.

These four bundles of fibers are in fact connected to each other through the power centers and govern their modulation. When, during the sequence, we come down with our hands along the front flows, as we move our hands along them we carry out a regulating action, integrating all of our perceptual possibilities.

The more our attention is refined at that moment, the greater the precision of this regulation and connection.

The lateral flows determine our stability in the time mode, or determine the precise attitude of the time mode. In very simple words, they can act on the slightest variation in the positioning of the assemblage point, making it stable.

This ability to stabilize depends on the fact that the two front flows are inserted in the time line; actually, they practically issue from it.

When we work well on the lateral flows we should feel right away firm, straight, and sturdy.

The time line

What I will say now about the time line is the attempt to describe something that has no way of being described through language. The time line can only be experienced. I count on the fact that these words can help you anyway as a guide to obtain the right sensations, the ones that will then bring you, eventually, to the pragmatic understanding of this aspect of the universe.

The Toltecs realized about the existence of a very particular earth line.

This power line is an aspect of energy, the one that actually gathers the possibility of organizing the emanations, the potential configuration of the alignments (that is, of the "worlds"). They called it the time line for two main reasons.

First of all, because they discovered that from it issues the possibility to control the time mode, the fundamental outcome of the assemblage point position. The assemblage point position, in fact, determines the time mode (or vice versa…). It is a matter of primary importance from the point of view of the seers; when they reached this understanding, they realized that they could control the assemblage point position with extreme precision by intervening directly on the time mode.

The second reason is that our eyes are hitched to this line; we are like hanging from it. All beings endowed with awareness are hitched to the flow of the time line and have potentially the power to affect the exact attitude of the line itself by "moving," "flowing" along it.

Depending on the way we use our eyes, the line reacts and we can move, slide, modifying the time mode itself. This is how the Toltects realized that the time line can be stimulated in the same way in which intent is evoked with the eyes; indeed, that it becomes a way thanks to which the time line and intent coincide, share the same space. This space of coincidence can be extended to infinity; when it happens, the Toltecs say they have "opened the time line."

In the sequence we use movements that are intended to open the time line.

A last remark:

Although it is called a "line," try to make an effort and not imagine it as a line that goes from a beginning to the end. Time is not linear, it is more similar to something "parallel in every possible direction." Above all, it cannot be thought but only experienced. It is called "line" only because the earth has the power to organize the possible alignments in a flow that allows the connection of conscious beings.

THE ROLLING FORCE

The rolling force is one of the most mysterious elements in the universe and is the source of incredible potential. It is strictly related to conscious beings, but it is also a direct propagation of the Eagle, not subject to the effects of the alignment, of any alignment. We can say that it goes through them all simultaneously in the essence of time.

The rolling force flows continuously over all living beings; it hits them, runs over them, and has fundamental effects on them. It has two aspects: one that arrives first and brings energy, inner force, awareness, clear direction; and a second aspect that arrives barely a moment after, practically almost together with the first. The latter has a disrupting effect on the emanations that make up the human beings and, in time, ends up prevailing, bringing them to death.

These two aspects, if balanced and used with aware precision, become the absolute means to perform ordinarily unconceivable maneuvers that concern the handling of the assemblage point and the access to the dark sea of awareness. It is one of the modern seers' most shattering discoveries, one with a cosmic reach. What actually substitutes every other means to access the unknown.

The new seers have made a science of it, a revolutionary part of their knowledge, equal to dreaming and stalking (and maybe more). Yet, using it for these purposes is extremely risky; that is why this part of their knowledge is reserved to extremely balanced warriors, devoid of self-absorption, endowed with a perfect, practical understanding of impeccability.

Apart from this, however, balancing the two aspects is essential in order to obtain strength, resilience, and clarity in daily life.

Since very ancient times, the Toltecs have looked for the way to obtain this balance; and the part of the sequence that concerns the rolling force is one of the results of these efforts.

I will add a fundamental suggestion: when Castaneda talks in his books about death being on our left, of the fact that one turns left to look at death and take advice, he refers exactly to the possibility of becoming aware of the existence of this force.

Similarly, it is what Don Juan talks about when he refers to the presence of something in the wind that is not wind and that reacts to our exposure to it or to our dodging it.

PREPARATION

THE ATTENTION ON THE BODY

This is a very special type of preparation, constantly applied by warriors in their daily life, aside from the practice of the sequence or any other practice.

It is a separate activity, fundamental (maybe the most important), but one that is necessarily and harmonically integrated in the process of learning the sequence.

We usually pay very little attention to our body conditions, to how we are moving, to the consequences (also in terms of heightened state) that ensue from the positions we assume, from the way we perform actions and, above all, to what ensues from the relationship between the use of attention and physical effort.

This is our “normal” condition, the one dominated by the inner dialogue. Warriors adopt a new condition. They cultivate it in time with great commitment, precision, and continuity, until it becomes practicable and stable, integrated with the common actions.

What they obtain in the end is to unify perception and physical action. I am not simply talking about paying attention to the way we move, to physical tensions, to body effort. Warriors carry out actions connecting and engaging perception in doing it.

It is the foundation of seeing: perceiving with the totality of ourselves. If the physical body and its acting are not involved in this process we will always be diminished and dominated by the inner dialogue.

The attention is continuous but endowed with the maximum relaxedness, softness, and force.

THE AREA OF POSSIBILITIES

In order to perform the sequence correctly, it is essential to learn to move in the area of possibilities up to the moment in which the movements connect with the will.

At that point, from the start, from the moment in which we go down toward the earth, we slide easily in the passages created between the bundles of emanations. These passages are the real spaces in which the sequence exists. Understand: the sequence already exists, we just follow its dynamics.

I will not repeat here the techniques to reach the area of possibilities, which I have already indicated in other books, shown in the videos and in workshops.

What I want to underline is that, if we are enclosed in the area of possibilities, the movements of the sequence are inserted in time, in the spaces determined by time that defines the space and speed of execution. This is a fundamental aspect of the sequence: it leads us to physically understand the nature of time.

Furthermore, the movements in the area of possibilities lead to lose the physical limits of our body, allowing us to involve the whole luminous egg, every layer of it.

When we acquire familiarity with the area of possibilities, we realize that "open" passages are created that exert a special attraction on the movement we are doing, as spaces of minor resistance in which we can slide or empty spaces that attract or push and guide the movements.

These passages are also called “continuity flows” because, once we are able to hitch them, we can flow in the area of possibilities without interruption and with absolute harmony.

The eyes, too, are involved in this state, as they are dragged by the attention into sensations of movements corresponding to the passages in which we execute the sequence.

It is the way in which the perception refines the exact attitude of the time mode.

We always do it to maintain the ordinary stability. It happens, for instance, every time we feel something, any feeling or emotion: our eyes refine the exact attitude of the time mode; except that we do it without awareness, automatically, without a possibility of choice.

Warriors use the eyes consciously; they know how to evoke particular conditions and states. For example, they can bring about inner silence only by modifying the light in their eyes, the way they are using them.

In this manner, we can select feelings and discover new ones, apply non-ordinary states of attention, amplify boundaries, tear limits down.

The sequence teaches to do it in the right way.

BREATHING

As you will see in the detailed explanation, the sequence develops a certain "respiratory form." It is associated with the movements but can also be carried out as a preparatory exercise in itself. Also, it clearly becomes a practice to all intents and purposes. If we learn to modulate our breathing exactly in the sequence, we can acquire a special control over our respiration. Learning to execute the breathing as a reiteration act, even disengaged from the movements, frees very precious quotas of energy and attention.

In the section dedicated to breathing you will find the whole breathing sequence described correctly.

PHYSICAL PREPARATION

If carried out in the proper way, the sequence also involves a great deal of physical exertion.

Or better: a correct, exacting, physical exertion. At the end of the execution it should be very clear. We feel that the whole body has worked a lot, but in a manner that brings vigor instead of weariness. The sensation of action, the result of the activity, is uniformly distributed in every single muscular fiber.

We feel loose, relaxed, but full of a special, serene force associated to clarity and patience.

There is a whole series of "preparatory exercises" that are fit to engage the body and put it in the ideal condition to perform the sequence in this way.

Actually, there is one for every movement of the sequence; each of these preparatory acts also works as a trigger to insert variants into the sequence, making it usually end in a different way than the usual. The variants' function is to orient the sequence toward specific intents.

However, it is impossible for me to insert all in this book, and I believe that it would just lead to creating huge confusion with respect to the main purpose, which is: learning the sequence correctly.

When you will have become a single thing with the state induced by the sequence, the variants will come of their own accord, together with the intent implemented by the generations of warriors who have preceded us. The key point in identifying the variants (which are potentially infinite) is to have understood that the sequence does not consist of a series of movements, but of a precise intent that, if sustained, produces a certain series of movements of the assemblage point.

It is this series of movements of the assemblage point that, in turn, generates the sensations that, applied to the area of possibilities, guide us to perform certain precise, physical movements.

The intent implemented by the sequence is that of the predominance of the energy body.

If we introduce a different intent in the execution of the sequence, also the assemblage point positions, the sensations, and the physical movements will take another course.

In short, all the real difficulty in learning the sequence lies in identifying and then maintaining a precise intent, in developing an unbending intent that is exactly defined.

I will suggest you some "actions" that are very useful in preparing for the sequence, both on the physical and on the other levels.

Moving in the area of possibilities with the right tension.

When you move in the area of possibilities, instead of looking for the continuity flows, that is, less resisting dynamics, you can focus on the areas of greater resistance and use them to obtain a type of elastic, physical tension that is very useful to fortify the body, endow it with a type of resistance that is not simply muscular.

Unifying the flow of continuity within the physical engagement.

Every time we use the body in some kind of physical engagement, we can exploit the chance to forge and fortify ourselves. Everything depends on how we use the attention, which also means that, if we move in the right way, we can unify physical action and perception, intensifying both.

The secret lies precisely in achieving the unity of the perception of the internal continuity flows with the act that we are performing.

It all starts from the area of possibilities and from the double perception. The material action must be parallel and matching, it must synchronize with the corresponding continuity flows. In this way, the state of attention is modified, what we do becomes acting for the sake of acting; we shift into the will. So, even the simplest gesture we make includes a type of strength that exercises body and attention.

Controlled rapid movements

As described below, in the part dedicated to the refinements, these consist in “charging” the control of the will while looking for the passages in the area of possibilities. Then we allow the body to spring, “gliding” in the open flow. However, this movement is immediately controlled by the discipline of the unbending intent that governs it by modulating the dynamic expression of the time mode in the movement itself.

Propulsive walk

See its description in the book about the recapitulation.

THE PREDOMINANCE OF THE ENERGY BODY

EXECUTION

In order to make its execution as clear as possible, the sequence has been divided into single movements. Every movement has a name, which is also indicated in the video (which you can find in the Internet) for the whole duration of the movement itself.

THE EARTH

When starting, as soon as we feel ourselves being pulled down by the earth (as we do the initial gazing), we crouch down already with the intent to sink into the earth.

We look for the sensation that connections are being created, lines or fibers that from our hands and arms go down into the earth and pull us down.

We are free to put the right or left leg in front and to hold our eyes either closed or open. There are no codified movements in this phase, but the knee does not rest on the ground.

This is an important detail, we have to be abandoned, but without ever letting ourselves go. Putting the knee on the ground to make less effort is already a sign of our indulging.

At the base of our feet there is a pool of greater density, of concentrated attention. It is a thickness that we have to perceive physically, to the touch. We slip our hands there, inside this thickness.

Initially, move this area with your hands, shifting the attention on the sensation of having your fingers inside something dense. You must not think it: you have to perceive it. Try doing it until it becomes a clear sensation.

In this first part of the sequence, what counts is mainly the intent to obtain that the earth lines lift and move the luminosity of this pool upwards. We hook the lines of the earth to those of the pool; the use of the hands helps us “intending” all of this.

With the fingers, we stimulate the earth until we hitch to its lines that help us lift this area of energy at the base of our feet, endowed with a higher density of attention and awareness, with a denser thickness.

The moment we feel we have welded the lines of the earth together with our own luminosity, we start pulling upwards. It is like having jelly all around us; we use our arms to keep our attention on the intent of lifting. This initial phase is important to fine-tune our attention, our ability not to lose our grip.

Partly, it is we who are lifting, partly it is the push coming from the earth that allows us to sustain and lift all. This makes it clear from the start that we need to have enough humbleness to accept help from the world.

It is a delicate work that must be felt physically; if we pay attention to our inner dialogue, we lose our ability to do it.

When the density rises, we continue pulling upwards, enveloping the whole body in such density until it closes above our head. As we sustain and lift, we find ourselves with the arms and then the whole body "inserted" in an energy structure that we have to continue to sustain.

It is the will that maintains and rules the process.

When we close above our head, we should feel a particular sensation, a sort of prickle or tingle that can also spread to the length of our spine.

Then we come down the front with our hands until we reach the area of the will, like sealing a zipper, in order to compact and define, stabilize what has been lifted. In this way we have obtained a more luminous cocoon, denser with awareness, and more silent.

THE DIRECTION

We stay with our hands in front of the will long enough for the attention to gather in the two areas of the peripheral vision (remember that we are looking ahead of us at the level of our eyes), down to the right and left.

At the exact moment when we feel or see that this attention has gathered, with a rotating movement we go to the vibratory center, latching again onto the earth lines as we pass with our hands through the two areas down to the right and left in our peripheral vision. So, we bring these quotas of attention toward the vibratory center.

For the whole duration of the sequence, remember that, if you are in the right state of attention, the movements have no break in continuity. They are all connected one to the other by means of the flows that are produced in our luminous egg while we move in this state.

Actual lines are being traced, and in time they become even visible. They are lines that the moving physical body produces in the depth of the luminosity and that are maintained in this luminous area around the physical body.

Now we light, with this movement, the vibratory center that gives us direction and clarity of action.

With this gesture we compact and channel it, so that it will not be dispersed: we have to perceive a flow coming out of our chest, lighting it physically. Furthermore, we have to feel that we hold with our hands this flow, a group of fibers, a force.

To succeed in this, we also have to find the right distance and positioning of the hands.

Make small adjustments until you find the exact position. The hands are firmly extended, creating a certain tension, but are relaxed.

Moreover, if we wait and guide our attention, we realize that such flow is connected to a center in the area of the shoulder blades and that there is a connecting passage that goes through our body, from the vibratory center to these "wings of perception." These are fibers that extend, stretch out from this zone in the back. Therefore, also this area is set in motion at the same moment in which a flow gets organized from the vibratory center.

The authentic discipline needed by a warrior is generated from the vibratory center.

THE CHANGE OF INTENSITY

We breathe in as we lift our arms; in this way, we create a window with our hands. These face each other and are held up straight, tense, with fingers united. Then we choose an area in front of us, at eye level; this becomes our gazing area.

Throughout the sequence, the eyes are used in a non-ordinary way and do not remain completely fixed; they must be active, mobile but soft, and include the peripheral vision as well.

Once we have stabilized the gazing area, we breathe out our inner dialogue with a long exhalation, modulated and controlled, through the window made with our hands. We use the breath to empty our mind; from now on, we maintain the inner silence, or at least we "intend" doing it.

This movement can also be repeated various times to obtain the maximum silence possible.

THE ATTENTION BEYOND THE LIMITS

Breathing in, we expand our attention, the arms and hands open: we extend outwards, onto the world as emanations outside, by means of our attention. We must use our hands to amplify our perception, that is, we hitch our sight, hearing, all of our perceptual systems to our spreading hands, extending our perception to the maximum possible limit, to the point where the hands are between seeing and feeling, and beyond.

The hands must remain at the level of the time line.

I have to overcome the habitual way of perceiving by looking, or the obsessive way, only focused on fragments of reality.

From now on, we are compact but at the same time expanded in a state of control and abandonment.

In this way, we hook onto the lines of the world, we wait for them. In the end, the hands rest on the time line; we feel it passing in our eyes and on the palms of the hands, which bend slightly to grasp it.

From this moment on, I also include the area of peripheral vision and listening to the sounds in my gazing.

In time, this extension of our perception becomes the extension of our whole body.

THE SENSITIVITY OF THE VIBRATORY CENTER

Now, I drag my expanded perception and the lines of the world toward the vibratory center, position them at the center of the chest, with the fingers sinking in, without touching the body.

I hitch to the fibers in that area and pull them upwards, thus expanding the vibratory center as well: during the extension, we also hook onto the points of intensification of awareness, located under the collarbones; we latch onto them and pull them.

I have to clearly feel that I am grabbing and extending fibers, lines, filaments that emanate from specific, well-definite points in my body.

This extension makes the vibratory center light up and extracts a line of intensity from the points under the collarbone.

Then the hands position themselves in the upper areas to the right and left, in the peripheral vision.

These areas are related to the vibratory center through perception: by moving the fingers I must feel their movement in the vibratory center. There is a correspondence.

The movement of the fingers is free; the question is finding the way of moving them, stimulating the vibratory center through the fibers that we have extended.

It is like making guitar strings resonate.

As I do this, I am still gathering lines of the world up high, this time, connecting and fixing them to the ones I have extended from myself. This allows me to amplify myself toward new directions; thus, it is possible to experience a sense of liberation, a greater possibility of movement, like freeing myself from something that was keeping me blocked.

Then, I come down with my fingers along these lines that I have extended, still maintaining the correspondence in the vibratory center. I repeat at least three times.
I breathe in while extending; I breathe out going toward the center.
The moment I reach the maximum extension of the arms and open my hands, I am at the limit of the luminous egg. At that point, the fibers of the vibratory center hitch to the emanations outside.

THE DISCIPLINE OF ACTIONS

The last time, with two fingers for each hand (index and middle fingers) I bring what I have gathered in the vibratory center, which is like a core of density, toward the center for decisions.
I use the fingers to fine-tune my perception, in order to be precise and careful, fine and not rough in my sensations. I have to maintain what I have gathered, and so I cannot be distracted and lose it.
In fact, I do not touch the body because the sensation is not physical; instead, I have to make the perception accurate. By doing so, I keep continuous control over the sensation and guide the discipline generated by the vibratory center toward the center for decisions.
It is indeed from the vibratory center that the right type of discipline and inner force issues.
When we reach the center for decisions, we have to perceive this core of density settling at the base of the throat.

PATIENCE

After that, we continue dragging this core of density over the two intensification points under the collarbones, and then over the right and left sides. As we come down by the sides, we should feel a more or less marked shiver in our back. To stimulate the release of this shiver, you can try gliding downward, pressing the back of your nails on the sides; as you go down, the shiver rises. Do it a few times to store the sensation; then repeat it without touching the body.

Remember that the right side is for dreaming and the left is for seeing.

Also keep in mind that the vibratory center disciplines dreaming and seeing. The more powerful, firm, is this area, the more your dreaming becomes organized, stable, devoid of interferences.

This fact is evident, for instance, when passing from one dream to another; that is, when changing assemblage point position. In that case, we necessarily have to use the vibratory aspect of energy as a guide and force that opens the passage.

It is also essential when one "jumps" to another total alignment, when one crosses that perceptual nothingness that separates one world from another. The guide and resource for making this transition is the vibratory center.

Now we pause over the lower part, under the ribs, to bring about a circulation between the will and the area of unbending intent, forming a "lifebelt" of perception and action around our waist. This connection goes through the body, too, joining the area surrounding the navel and that of the kidneys in the back (the area of unbending intent).

The sensation is precisely of being run through by a flow, while a thicker density envelops us at the level of the sides.
Everything we have put in motion up to this point pours into this area; therefore, the hands must be firm and tense in order to govern this flow, with thumbs and little fingers extended. We keep the position until a clear connection between will and unbending intent is established.

THE PREPARATION

I come down with my hands, passing over the sartorius muscles (intensification points), then over the inner thighs (where there is a channel of intensity between the adductor muscles), then over the knees, going down to the feet.
The legs contain the memories, and the knees, if stimulated, connect with the memory storage in the legs (including the memories of dreaming and of the energy body), coordinating them.
Then I repeat this route backwards. After having connected everything again in the earth, I pull upwards, dislodging what is blocked, and arrive at the “lifebelt” again.
I must always maintain the vision of the moving lines to drag and reorganize our resources.

CALLING FORTH THE WORLD

I extend outward everything I have connected and gathered; when I turn my hands (palms facing outwards), I launch toward the world, intended as emanations outside. I make a circle with hands, arms, and shoulders.

I do this to start a process of reconfiguration of my energetic state. What I am trying to do, the intent that supports this and all of the moments in which, in the course of the sequence I "turn outwards", is to realign myself correctly with the world.

Indeed, a process takes place in humans that deeply alters their natural energetic configuration. All conscious beings carry out their internal alignment by orienting their energy fibers outward, coinciding with infinity. However, in human beings, because of self-absorption, the fibers twist, ending up self-reflecting, stiffening in a blocked position, stuck one against the other.

This is also the origin of our dullness and of the fact that our personal convictions become our masters, as well as the utmost advantage for the suggester.

Therefore, warriors seek to regain their natural alignment in every way, thus responding to infinity and connecting with intent. Continuing to stay disconnected means to remain in the zone of death while still living: our awareness becomes limited.

When I turn my hands outwards, it must be clear that I am emitting a wave of intensity.

Now, then, I wait for the consequent return wave from the world. I receive it, welcoming it on my hands extended forward, but its effect is clearly perceived by the will. In order to perceive the exact moment at which it comes, I have to project my attention, launch it forward, so as to provoke the world to respond; then, apply patience and maintain my pressure on the world.

RECEIVING THE WORLD

As soon as this return wave arrives from without, I accompany it inside, distributing this availability of power over the will, vibratory center, and center for decisions. The return wave gives a boost, and I use it right away, coordinating with its speed, implementing timing.

Then, I align again with the world at the level of the will and, like earlier, I wait for the return wave. With forearms and hands stretched out, and elbows bent at the sides, I receive the answer from the emanations outside. This response "rests" on the arms and is received directly by the will.

In this part of the sequence, this inside/out alignment, the search for the right configuration, reproduces the first part of the apprenticeship; as I was saying, we try to obtain the correct realignment of the emanations inside, and it is always done by looking for the collaboration, the help from the world.

THE DISCIPLINE OF UNBENDING INTENT

The return wave is brought back to the vibratory center. Then, again, pull the fibers up from the vibratory center and come back down with the hands.

Repeat the same step of bringing the discipline toward the center for decisions, then on the intensification points under the collarbones, over the right and left sides, and then sustain the connection between the will and unbending intent. This time, however, our hands move behind, to the area of unbending intent, and then down over the back of our thighs, knees, and calves. We come back up following the same path and sustain the lumbar connection.

In this way, I tie unbending intent to the earth lines and vice versa. This is very important, because the earth acts as a safe guide to non-ordinary directions and positions of the assemblage point that need the application of unbending intent in order to be sustained.

Remember that, when we hold our hands up by our sides, we have to wait for the necessary time for all that has been freed to reach this area and settle. We realize when this happens if we pay attention to the sensation of being crossed by a current, a flow between the belly and the back.

INNER STRENGTH

Now I extend everything along the line of the vibratory center; I rest my hands above the flow emanating from this center, I support and am supported by the direction contained in it.

The arms are relaxed, the hands are literally resting on the flow. I have to modulate the vibratory center by moving my hands in an almost imperceptible way. The sensation is that something is flowing under the hands, starting from the chest.

By moving the hands correctly, I can control the sensation that this flow transmits to the vibratory center; then, I use the variation of this sensation to find the right intensity.

The left hand is under the right, I modulate with my hands in order to govern the flow: this is what connects me to the direction of my existence; it is the path with a heart.

When I feel I have obtained the ideal regulation, a sensation of inner strength, I concentrate and push it inside. As I approach the vibratory center, I cross the hands in the image of a butterfly.

I come closer, but have to leave the right space between hands and chest (I have to find the correct distance through small adjustments with my hands), in order to allow the accumulation of a special force that "lights me up." This is the seat of inner strength.

Furthermore, accumulating force in the vibratory center connects us to the intent of the generations of warriors that have preceded us.

If you search images of Tula Atlases, you will see that they carry this butterfly on their vibratory center.

CONTROL

I wait, allow it to become denser, and when the density is enough, I push it toward the will, where I let it settle. I do this to make the second attention usable: the will, in fact, is the center that governs the second attention, but it needs to be disciplined, and this discipline is obtained from the vibratory center.

THE INFALLIBLE GUIDE

So, I begin governing the will; I grab the edges with my fingers and extend laterally. I must feel that I am pulling fibers at its sides, have this sensation directly in the belly. I use the filaments I have extended to connect the will to the lines of the earth, which must become their guide. I aim at trusting blindly the will and what it communicates, that is, its commands ensuing from our coinciding with intent.

The two areas below, right and left of the peripheral vision, are directly connected with the will. So, now I can tie it to the lines of the earth with an externally rotating movement; the movement is transmitted to the will. The connection must be concrete and also involve the right and left sides in order to dominate dreaming and seeing.

Accordingly, I will then bring this connection to the sides in order to get the second attention's mastery over dreaming and seeing; and then again, I extend it toward the world. With hands open and palms up, the fibers of the right and left sides extend toward the world: this lessens self-absorption in the second attention.

Again, I pull the strings from the will, grasp them with my thumb, ring and little fingers joined to get a "strong grip." With the remaining fingers I form a hook, which I use first to turn inwardly, various times, and then to hook outwardly with one single, last turn.

I bring it back to the sides, again strengthening the connection with the lines of the earth: this causes the earth to guide me in dreaming and seeing in safe positions and directions, related to freedom. I insert the connection in the flow of the will toward the world, then open my hands and receive the world again.

Finally, I pull again laterally and do then a "test" to verify if the connection with the earth is effective. I apply pressure to the two lower points of the peripheral perception; if the connection exists, I will feel the pressure I am exerting directly in the body, on my belly. In order to receive this signal, one needs to pay extreme attention.

The earth is an infallible guide.

THE REALIGNMENT

I go back over the sides to involve the dreaming and seeing, dragging there the connection I have obtained; then I extend again along the direction of the vibratory center, this time putting the right hand underneath the left. Like earlier, I modulate and then do the butterfly, densify, and concentrate the inner strength.

This time, however, once the right density between the hands and the vibratory center has been reached, I hook it, claw it with my fingers. Then, maintaining this hold, I extend the fibers as I extract them, and turn them outwards. Also in this case, the intent is to extend toward infinity.

Again, I wait for a wave to return from the world; it is like a light thrust that settles between my hands.

It is the moment in which I mostly change the direction of my fibers' orientation, coinciding with the world. In this moment, I uphold to the utmost my fight against self-absorption, also because I do it with the vibratory aspect.

The sensation of changing direction, of turning the involved fibers outwardly, must be perceived physically.

The effect spreads throughout my whole energy configuration, on my alignment. I extend myself not only from the vibratory center, but also from my whole being.

We are actually on our confines; the world receives our pressure made of attention and responds. The answer is a return wave that can also be visual or tactile.

If the extension succeeds and there is an answer, this return wave, made of silence, comes from the world. I grasp it, bring it toward myself, settling it on my vibratory center, and this gives me compactness. We are simultaneously extended and compact, and thus resistant.

Then I drag the expanded world onto the will, making discipline, inner force, and control coincide; and this again helps fighting self-absorption.

Moving on in the sequence, we become increasingly shifted on the will, and it becomes impossible for us to do these things by thinking them; it is essential to intend them.

They are perceived and intended.

EXTENDING UNBENDING INTENT

Now, with the world's complicity, I shape the will, manipulating it; I mould its density, adjust it to the emanations of the earth. I make sure that the will's fibers absorb the type of discipline generated by the agreement between the vibratory center and the emanations at large. This is preparatory for the extension of unbending intent, given the correlation between the latter and the will.

I slide over my sides up to the zones of the peripheral vision down to the right and left; again, I hitch to the lines of the earth with a turn of my hands and then reach the area of unbending intent.

From there, every time I repeat this movement I create a final connection between all of the centers, the lines of the earth, and the world as emanations outside.

To do it, I latch onto unbending intent, grasp its fibers (again, without touching the body) and extend them toward the world, guiding them first alongside the will, then the vibratory center, and finally the center for decisions, always passing over the right and left sides. Every time I come back toward the area of unbending intent, I follow the same course backwards, dragging and settling the emanations outside.

I must feel with clarity the continuity created while I do the movements, maintaining it at every instant. These movements also help to "comb" the fibers of unbending intent, giving us a sense of greater stability and clarity.

So, through the interaction between unbending intent and the perception areas I can exactly coincide with the current alignment, no matter what alignment it is.

This means that I extend my emanations inside on the ones at large and stabilize the position or the direction of the assemblage point; or I apply an unbending intent in any position or direction.

For example, if I do this extension in my dreaming, it gets stabilized, because, through unbending intent, I align correctly with the new position.

In short, I do this to confirm and select the alignment, in order for the coincidence with the alignment in which I am to be precise. This improves the ability to control the movement or the stability of the assemblage point.

The movement is repeated two more times, first at the level of the vibratory center and then of the center for decisions. I must glide my hands along the sides with great precision, not carelessly, arriving at the exact level of the vibratory center and then of the center for decisions before moving the hands forward.

THE OPENING

Once the center for decision has been reached, I grasp it in the center, inside the line separating the right and the left sides, then I pull outward, opening the arms, also pulling on the lines of the intensification points below the collarbone, at the level of which the hands turn and push outward, on both sides, creating a space, expanding it.

I must really push the two sides of the luminous egg apart. This is the intent.

The exact sensation is that I extend and open, separate the right and left sides. In this way, I increase my maneuvering space, my possibility within the current alignment to amplify myself beyond the limits of the normal, starting position. My perception should slightly modify the moment I open.

The intent is to create a minimal opening between the right and left sides and, starting from the center for decisions, I can thus increase my ability to make totally voluntary and free choices.

I avail myself of this opening also to evoke the intent of seeing; to help myself, I almost join my hands, leaving some space between one and the other; and when I bring them toward the face I cross my eyes, looking in the space between them.

The sensation is of pushing myself forward thanks to the crossed eyes and of passing beyond the perceptual barrier, like when I am falling asleep.

In fact, our eyes cross at the moment of falling asleep.

This happens because of the mobility acquired by the assemblage point while we are falling asleep.

THE LINES OF FORCE

My hands move over the head; I should feel a tingling sensation on the top of my head at every passage. I must look for this sensation actively, and stabilize it so as to find it again in the course of the sequence.

An excellent way to stimulate it consists in walking under a mirror placed at a certain distance above the head.

Now I grasp the fibers in the area of the shoulder blades; it is like grabbing their tip. I must search attentively until it is clear that I caught something issuing from the area around the shoulder blades and that I can extract, free it. This zone is endowed with high sensitivity and able to govern perception that, in fact, is modified as I maneuver and latch onto these fibers.

By doing so, I open the wings of perception; I spread the fibers that I pull, drag over my head, and place in the two front flows, in two very important channels that sustain us and connect every center. I come down along these vertical bundles of fibers to the two intensification points of the sartorius muscle. At this moment, too, it is necessary to be very perceptive; we are connecting the back and the front; the perception must light up all of the body's points during the passage.

As I come down, I must get the physical correspondence of the different points, on the front and in the back. There are, in fact, two other bundles of fibers in the back, corresponding to the ones in the front.

While I come downwards, settling the heightened perception that I have extracted from the area of the shoulder blades (from the wings of perception), I must intend this correspondence and the front-back connection for the various centers: eyes – time line, vibratory center – wings of perception, will – area of unbending intent, and right and left sides. During the descent, the sensation should be similar to letting a fluid physically flow inside us.

This movement requires a great deal of precision in the use of attention, and the most detailed perception of the whole body.

These four lateral flows (front and back) give us stability, strength, and balance if they are compact, united and connected in a clear, lucid way.

The motion followed as we come down could have a rather wavy, serpentine progression. Let the hands follow something that exists in reality.

The movement ends at the level of the lower intensification points. Here, I gather a pure unit of intent, resulting from the previous maneuvers, and can decide what to use it for.

THE CHANGE IN DIRECTION

With the hands almost united at the fingertips, I lift the unit of intent up to the center for decisions. I place it in the center, releasing the specific intent in which I have decided to engage it. This specific intent will make sure that I take a precise direction with respect to it.

I insert the fingers between the two halves, right and left, at the level of the center for decisions and open the arms like before, pushing toward the two sides, as though I opened two sliding doors. I do it to increase my available space. I obtain this space by opening the two sides. Remember to maintain the peripheral vision.

The sensation I am looking for is that a real opening is created in front of me.

To exploit straightaway the larger space I have obtained, I immediately change the direction of my inner alignment: head to the right, right hand protecting the area of the will, left hand up, at the level of the time line, with the palm facing outwards.

These two gestures allow me to abandon myself to seeing.

The sensation that should be looked for when I turn to the right is that my eyes are looking into an immense space, independently of what is materially in front of me. In this space I evoke intent. I am abandoned but control what is happening in other directions; therefore, the hands move in protection, stopping every intrusion, and I can release the seeing.

The gaze is slightly crossed to penetrate the barrier of interpretation.

OPENING THE LEFT SIDE

I turn my head forwards; the left arm slashes with the hand edgewise, at eye level, on the time line. I must insert it in a sort of natural seam at the limit of the luminous egg that exists at the extreme border of our peripheral vision: it is this seam that allows us to open the left side.

The sensation we are looking for is that the hand is lodged in a slot that is already present, a precise space where the seam begins.

The right hand moves to the side, aiming downwards and creating a sort of tripod with thumb, index, and middle fingers. This I need to be firm and create a contrast by keeping the right side solid through this support on the earth, while the left side "melts."

Then, the left hand starts gliding, going down the seam I just mentioned. The hand must go down naturally; it has to glide down this slot of its own accord, not following a straight line but a slightly serpentine path. To help us, we let the hand glide down as we are breathing out.

We enter then with our hand under the layers of the luminous egg and extend all the fibers. As it goes back up, the hand must be inserted in the layers that are closest to the physical body.

It is necessary to identify the sensation of lightly ungluing the layers and introducing the hand, raising it through the layers and, when we extend it outwards, increase the separation.

We repeat the movement a few times, until we feel the left side becoming fluid. Every time we do it the sensation must really be that our left side melts, becomes liquid, merges with the world.

There is not a fixed number of times for this movement. We repeat it until the sensation of openness becomes clear.

Then we change the direction in which we operate. We hold our hand still below and make it rise slowly with a well-perceivable updraft, which is connected with the boost of the earth and the ability to distinguish places of coincidence. Therefore, we wait for this rising current to come.

It is something light but substantial that lifts the hand, makes it float.

To help ourselves, we allow the hand to rise as we breathe in; our breathing connects with this boost from the earth. Once up, we go down as we insert our hand between the layers closest to the body and extend the left side a few times, like we did a moment ago. This time, however, we come in from above, from the head down, and expand the left side on the whole trunk.

It is a fundamental moment: the sensation of opening the left side favors the shift of the assemblage point inwardly, in the direction of the vibratory center.

Conversely, every time the assemblage point moves toward the vibratory aspect of energy, the first thing we feel is that our left side melts. So, we can cause this movement by evoking the right sensation.

This type of movement contributes enormously to getting rid of the human form, because it is an inward movement to the left.

To give you an idea of the capacity of this type of movement, know that the fire from within takes place exactly when the assemblage point coincides exactly with the core of the vibratory center.

Actually, the left side does not really open. The sensation that we achieve, of being without limits, melted, one with the world on the left side, depends on a characteristic of that seam. By evoking the correct sensation, this seam becomes softer, a less hard area and, immediately, merges the emanations inside with the emanations at large, outside. We translate this energy fact into the sensation of being open on the left side.

THE GAZE BEYOND INTERPRETATION

We now put our left hand edgeways before our left eye; the right eye looks ahead. Thus begins an operation for the differentiation between the right and left eyes, which also continues in the subsequent steps and which is important to see clearly.

We turn left with the arm and head, then we extend the arm. As the arm is being extended, we have to look at the hand, follow it and use it as a springboard, a runway to launch the gaze beyond the hand, toward infinity. Initially, the eyes are crossed as they fixate on the hand's edge; then, following it as it is extended, they revert to the normal eyesight, until, the instant the hand lowers completely, the gaze darts away.

We look into an endless corridor, toward a distance beyond conceivable, which is not in the ordinary time but beyond the bonds of interpretation.

This is a key moment, the way we use our eyes is decisive, therefore we must wait a moment, give time to allow our sight to release the force that is waiting down there. So, we are already evoking the rolling force to prepare the subsequent moments. The exact moment we perceive something taking off and starting from this infinite distance, we turn, facing forward again.

EXPANDING THE LEFT SIDE

As soon as I turn forwards the hand goes to the left eye to grab some very important fibers and extend them along the time line. In fact, our eyes are always connected to the time line; the way they fixate or not in this connection determines the exact time mode, that is, the alignment and position of the assemblage point. In other parts of the sequence, too, we will see how to intervene to free the innate possibilities of the connection with the time line. As I explain the breathing section below, the sensation tied to this gesture must be fine-tuned with great precision.

When we get at the end of the extension, we open the hand and let go what we have gathered along this line. What we must feel is that something is released from the left eye and extends without limit; we have to get to perceive that we grasp the fibers and extract them from the eye. These fibers go through our body, starting from the will and coming out of the eye laterally.

Once the correct sensation is obtained, we use the same procedure coming down to the various fundamental centers (decisions, vibratory, will) and extend them toward infinity.

THE PROTECTED STANCE

The left hand is open facing forward at eye level; I lean on the time line and push it. I must really push; the hand stays still, the rest of the body moves backwards on the left leg, while the right hand, still forming a tripod, turns backward to support itself.

Thus, I find myself standing slightly behind with respect to the opening made on the left side. This is a protected position that allows me not to be completely exposed: the opening allows us to access the rolling force's options, but we do not stand exactly on the line of fire. It is like moving "behind the corner."

THE ROLLING FORCE – Preparation

We turn 90 degrees to the left by simply sliding on our feet.

This time, we touch our body with the right hand. The fingers must enter the spaces between the ribs, on the dreaming side; this physical stimulus is needed to help us maintain integrity, and in these conditions, it is easier on the side of dreaming. The legs are firm and active; consider that you have to hold the boost or the jerk (so, you do not know well in what direction you will be jolted) by a force endowed with its own will.

The left hand protects the vibratory center, to keep our vital force compact, together. This is essential; therefore, before starting the next movements, we wait for the area included between the hand and the vibratory center to become sufficiently dense. It must fill up until it becomes gluey.

First, we have opened the left side to make the assemblage point move inwardly, in the direction of the vibratory center, in order to put ourselves in a more resilient, lucid, quicker, and more perceptive position. The way we use our eyes in this phase is important.

As soon as I turn, I use the eyes to entice the rolling force and look into the infinite corridor that I have prepared before. The gaze must go beyond, going through anything I have before me; it must breach through interpretation in order to call the rolling force from what appears as an endless distance.

Now we are suspended in an eternal moment, which is that of the rolling force and emanations at large, which are always present, without or through time as we know it or as we do not know it.

This is how we look: going beyond everything, through solidity. Because the time line coincides with us in this moment, we have turned to face time, and before us is the rolling force. There is nothing but the time of the rolling force coming toward us.

We wait for the vision/perception of something coming from an immense distance; at this moment, neither before nor after, with our right hand we anticipate the rolling force's movement by an infinitesimal fraction and start harmonizing ourselves with the it through a coordinated movement.

However, just a moment before inserting the right hand in the rolling force's motion, I expand my space by forcefully pushing with the left hand. With the inner part of the hand I drag the density of the vibratory center, which is what should determine the range and stability of this expansion. With the external part, the back of my hand, I move something that opposes resistance.

The right hand starts tracing a clockwise, conic spiral that goes down, with its tip, to the right side. Here, it is particularly important to perceive the area of possibilities; we have to recognize the right time as we rotate and direct something that opposes a certain resistance.

First, we start rotating beyond the left hand, which stands as protection; we take and bring toward us with this spiraling movement.

In this way, we create a fine-tuning with the rolling force, a cavity, a deformation of the layers of the energy fibers that allows us to hook onto and coordinate with the rolling force itself.

The formation of this cavity will be fundamental at the end of the sequence, when we will use it again to make the attention of the energy body coincide with that of the physical body.

Then we push the left hand outwards, like before, feeling the resistance and creating, piece by piece, a larger and safe space for ourselves. The first spiral ends with only one inner rotation. Then, as we create more and more space, we increase the number of internal rotations with respect to the rotations beyond the left hand. The right hand positions itself again on the side pulling back, like creating an eddy.

In this way, I create a modification in our energy configuration, which later on will permit me to follow the same speed as the rolling force. It is a niche suited to host the right point of the rolling force.

The intent is to harmonize with the rolling force's speed, dynamics, and type of movement.

THE ROLLING FORCE – Harmonization

With my gaze I call again the rolling force. The sensation is still that something very powerful is coming from over there, at the end. It is a force, but what we feel is that it is endowed with its own intentionality. We face the rolling force only when we clearly obtain this perception: it is a force endowed with intentionality, an abstract, impersonal intentionality.

Now I use the niche I created earlier, in the previous part of the sequence, to hitch to the rolling force's motion.

I have to wait for the perception, the sensation of this incoming motion. It really comes toward us like a big wheel with a precise speed and uniform, perpetual motion.

We hook onto it, that is, we hitch to this already ongoing movement, like catching a running train. It is the will that decides the exact moment, we have to trust it absolutely. So, we can follow the rolling force's motion, continuously controlling our state in order to remain settled in the point chosen by the will.

The rolling force's blows usually damage us because our rigidity opposes resistance; but now we have its same dynamics. Thus, the rolling force's speed does not harm us; actually, it becomes a vehicle. In this way, our cocoon does not suffer any impact.

The arms harmonize with an alternate movement; then they align and move together when this harmonization is right and can accompany our exit from the line of the rolling force.

Obviously, we are the ones who have to adapt to the rolling force's motion, and not the opposite.
The application of patience and timing in this part of the sequence is essential.

NOT INDULGING

Now we break loose; we suddenly turn to obtain final control over this maneuver; or better, the final control on the ability to avoid indulging in general.
The way we do this turn to the right is important. The idea is that I have to close an airtight door, completely shift the attention in an instant. The movement must be clear-cut, strong, decisive, but harmonious, fluid, precise, and soft.
It is a controlled rapid movement.
I have attained control over the ability to shift the attention; in other words, I can always move away from the line of fire, not only with the rolling force, but also with every thing.
These are exactly the sensation and intent.
The right hand moves edgeways in front of the face. The left hand is placed edgeways on the same line below, more or less at the level of the will. As soon as I position the right hand, I cross my eyes at once as I look at the edge of the hand, then I return to the normal vision. This variation stimulates us to shift the attention effectively, totally; in short, not to indulge.
We feel at once straight, firm, and compact: it is a form of final control.

THE MANEUVERABILITY OF THE VIBRATORY ASPECT

Now I come down with the right hand and come up with the left. While I breathe in deeply, the two hands pass one above and the other below the vibratory center following a diagonal trajectory. The hands keep a certain distance from each other when they glide over the vibratory center. There must be a certain thickness: the force we have developed in the previous part of the sequence.

What I am looking for with this action are new directions. The vibratory center governs the force that directs us, that guides our existences, but is normally blocked in one single direction. It is the one we have taken as the compulsory consequence of our personal history and of the coercive force of the human form: it is a direction taken without the possibility to choose.

So now we stretch, extend, spread the fibers from the vibratory center so as to include many other of its possibilities; we amplify the horizon from a limited vision to the entire horizon, with the possibility of choosing now, as we execute the movement.

I push the extension of the vibratory center. On one side, the right hand pushes down, toward the earth, palm down. On the other side, toward the time line, the left hand holds this line that passes through the eyes and causes the fibers of the vibratory center to be inserted and to flow in the time line itself.

The body posture must always be firm and strong.

After the inspiration, which I do during this extension phase, now, while remaining in the position I reached, I breathe out slowly accompanying the whole exhalation with a particular movement of the eyes.

I make my gaze glide slowly along the diagonals from up and right, going down to the left and vice versa (from up and left, going down to the right); first along the diagonal where I do not have my hands, and then on the one where my hands are positioned. The exhalation is single and uninterrupted during both routes; so it must be very controlled and modulated. The eyes must look with continuity, without spurts or interruptions; they must follow the diagonal line uniformly, catching every detail, following depth planes, gliding over the surface of what they meet without losing contact. We use the eyes to look for new opportunities, new directions.

It is essential that the will participates actively to this way of looking; actually, it is thanks to the will that our eyes stay glued to the pathway. If we succeed in attaining the state of connection eyes-will, we immediately get a much deeper inner silence and the ability to find effective directions.

The same procedure is repeated by inverting the hands, again vertically, and then on the horizontal line at the level of the vibratory center, thus producing the total extension of the vibratory center. In the last movement the gaze must be led along the diagonals and then also horizontally. Every time we switch, the hands realign along the front line, while the eyes cross; then they slide over the vibratory center, accompanied by a deep inhalation.

The described breathing manner forms the control of the new directions, while the way of using the eyes allows us to find these new directions, examining the world's details with continuity. Changing the way we use the eyes is essential; it determines the real change in the use of our attention.

All this work is tied to stalking; it must provide us maneuvering spaces that we can use also in everyday life to operate new choices. Our body can remember the useful directions and resort to them during the course of daily actions or non-ordinary actions.

OPENING THE TIME LINE

Hands opposed on the frontal area, the left over the center for decisions, the right under the will, preparing, gathering.

Now, first the right and then the left hand rise, moving toward the shoulder blades to grab the wings of perception. As I pass over the head, I should feel a light tingling or slight irritation on the top of my head. Then, I go behind.

I have to actively search in the area above the shoulder blades until I feel that there is something to grab; I do it by paying a great deal of attention to my perceptual state (I am still gazing). Indeed, when I "grab" the right fibers, two main things must happen: the first is to feel the area of the shoulder blades being pulled; the second is that my way of looking at and perceiving what I have in front of me changes. This change takes place both in the way I use and feel the eyes and in the quality of my perception that becomes more intense, lucid, deeper, but also different from normal, somehow altered. It can consist of minimal variations that require high sensitivity, much inner silence, patience, kindness, and timing. These are the best, because they make us become precise.

I drag these fibers I have grabbed, bringing them to eye level, passing over my head, then I stop and release them along the two frontal flows I had activated before.

I feel them descending, sliding along the frontal flows, down to the lower intensification points. I must feel that I am actually succeeding in extending and connecting these fibers.

Now I insert the hands in the time line and stay, watching the horizon created by the hands for the time needed to have the sensation of an endless spread in front of me. Then I expand myself, opening the arms and, sliding with my hands into the time line, I extend it. At the end of the opening, I find myself looking into a limitless horizon; before me, distributed in this horizon, I have the time modes, that is, the assemblage point positions, or dreaming positions.

Upon opening, before my eyes, a mist should form and then expand as we open our arms. The forming of this mist gives us the right opening time.

As we open the hands, the will is pulled and expanded along the time line; it is the participation of the will that allows the precise perception of the time modes that are spread in front of us.

THE TIME NICHE

Now I quickly crouch down, squatting: left leg in front, the right one back, left arm in front, the right hand on the right side (dreaming side). The fingers of the right hand enter the spaces between the ribs and under the ribcage. It is another of the moments in which we touch physically. We do it to have compactness.

The left hand in protection and the adopted position are needed to maintain a condition of extreme readiness. The knees must not touch the ground, precisely because we have to be very elastic and ready to spring, to oppose strength.

While doing this, we have gone down and settled in one of the time modes, in essence, into a dreaming niche, chosen by us. In this new position, we have to create and maintain all the maneuvering space we need, avoiding above all any interference from unwelcome visits. Therefore, we adopt this position and charge ourselves up.

Once we are sufficiently charged up, we get up by pushing with the right leg and the whole body. It must be like pushing against something and creating a space with this shove forward. We get up and go back down again, inverting the position; right hand in front and left on the seeing side. This way, we push away all interference, we sweep it away, as we make ourselves able to change alignment under the guide of the vibratory aspect.

While I am squatting, I must use the eyes in a special way. With my gaze, I catch some details around me, at least three or four. It is much better if these are immaterial details, like reflections of light, shades, or empty spaces between objects.

When I change side, I pick up the same details again. My gaze must jump from one to the other, but with extreme precision and firmness; that is, by making a real jump from one point to the next one; yet, upon reaching the new detail, the gaze blocks exactly and immediately, obtaining lucidity at once. I keep my hold on the detail for a short time and then move on to the next. This type of gaze serves to stimulate the dreaming attention, to train maintaining or changing position, and to control intrusions.

TIMING OR THE STALKER'S HARMONY

I get up aligning myself again, taking a very firm stance. The right hand is positioned with the palm down over the intensification point that is under the collarbone. The left hand presses the sartorius muscle with the fingertips. In this way, I create a special, diagonal connection between the intensification points and the right and left sides that provides me with the attention suited to pick up the changes in intensity around me.

My legs are bent but firm, grounded to the earth and active, mobile.

What I do now is to stalk quotas of attention and energy endowed with a high degree of effectiveness. I look ahead, but the attention must be kept down to the left in the peripheral vision, in the area connected to the will. I have to wait for something to happen in that zone. We can perceive a fleeting shadow, a spot of color or light, a nucleus of density, or a command like "now!" arriving from the will. It is the will that decides when and how to act. In the exact moment in which this command arrives, we have to dart and grab something in that zone.

It is an impulse that we have to learn to receive clearly and follow without any doubts; it must pure action.

This is a central moment, because it puts together all of the founding aspects of stalking: acting for the sake of acting, forbearance, timing, control, discipline. Thus, it is a moment for regulating stalking itself and harmony between actions and decisions.

In this phase it is essential that we are already shifted on the will as a reflection of intent and we need the total suspension of the interference by the inner dialogue, as well as unconditional trust in the will.

The fine-tuning of the principles of stalking is obtained and applied in this part of the sequence and extended to the subsequent part, in order to stabilize and keep these principles active for the rest of the sequence. When the change or command to act comes, we must be fast but precise; so, we coordinate with the will, we already confide in the energy body's capacity for action.

We allow the body to move, the hand to grab well, with precision and care, the availability of the peripheral area; then, we distribute the whole on the right side, the will, and coming up to the vibratory and decision centers, and again to the side.

We repeat on the other side, switching the hands' position.

This is also one of the moments in which we coordinate with intent. We wait for the will's command because we wait for the connection with the active side of infinity; we learn to become available to intent.

In this phase, we also look for the warrior's humbleness, because to become available to spirit means to free ourselves of power and of the sense of almightiness that one meets on the way to knowledge.

We are equal to the rest of the world since, in the moment when we are available to intent, we have no personal desires.

THE PRINCIPLES OF STALKING

As I said earlier, the physical application of the principles of stalking becomes stable in this phase. So, like in the previous part, we enact a well-balanced mix of control, discipline, forbearance, and timing. These elements are needed to choose the exact moment in which to act. We must not act too early nor too late, but only when the possibilities have accumulated at the right level and before they start vanishing; that is, when forbearance has accumulated resources and attention.

So, I must act like before: responding to the will's command in the precise instant in which it comes. It is my whole body that does it; I must be shifted on the will, excluding the interference from the inner dialogue. This way of acting also allows me to finally shift the attention from the ordinary mind to the will.

We put both hands on the sartorius muscles; we stimulate them by keeping a right, modulated pressure. The attention is on the lower areas of the peripheral vision to the right and left. We wait for the moment and then we go down to grab on both sides.

We spread what we found on the sides, then push everything downwards, into the earth and the pool of luminous awareness. We connect all of this work to the earth to obtain a stable connection with it in relation with the principles of stalking. It is like grabbing some handles that drag with them a nucleus of intensity.

Finally, we pull upwards, we launch, extend the connection through our layers and those of the earth…and beyond. This sudden extension also obtains the effect of discomforting the suggester, flinging it off, at least for a moment.

When we get up and as we launch upwards, the gaze is forward, it does not follow the hands. This contrasts with our tendency to let ourselves go; it increases aware discipline.

THE QUOTAS OF ATTENTION

Again, I go and get the fibers from the area of intense perception in the upper part of the back, the area of the shoulder blades. As I said before, I must search with accuracy, patience, and refined attention, until the movement of the fingers, our way of searching and grasping, determines a change, even small, in our state.

It could be a change in the way we are using perception, maybe in the colors, in the intensity of the sounds, in the planes of depth, or other. Or we realize that by touching something, back there, we feel different.

In that moment, I grab the fibers and drag them, without losing them, in front of me, at the level of the time line, and let them go inside the two frontal flows.

Then, once more, I create the horizon with the hands under my eyes.

I look ahead, but keep my attention on the extremities of the time line, right and left, in the peripheral vision. I wait…wait; something must change at the extremities of the time line, something that releases the impulse, the command to grab the quotas of attention located along the time line, just at the limits of the luminous egg but that come from much farther beyond.

These are other, very important quotas of attention, also because they are related with our latent possibilities.

In fact, after capturing them, we bring them to the center for decisions and wait until it is clear that everything has been absorbed in the body; precisely, through the center for decisions.

Also, pay attention to what takes place in the upper intensification points, because now, at that level, a new line gets activated that goes through us and that we use for the next passage.

In fact, now I stay with my hands on the vibratory center and wait again for the variation that releases intensity. Therefore, the attention is slightly below, in the peripheral vision, but at the level of the intensification points.

Again, I allow the attention to get charged up and receive the right moment; when it comes, I hitch these quotas of attention to the extremities of the line that goes through the center for decisions and bring them to the vibratory center. I wait for the latter to absorb everything and distribute it inside the body, like a fluid that spreads.

THE FINE-TUNING

I do a rotating movement downward, one hand facing the other. I must feel the density in the space and, as soon as I start, the will gets activated.

The sensation I am looking for, that I need to pay attention to, is the will's reaction, which gets turned on as soon as I start descending.

An exact correspondence is created between the vibratory center and the will. This descending and rotating movement is a real fine-tuning of the body and of the relationship between these two centers.

THE SPACE FOR THE NEW POSITIONS

Once I arrive on the will, I still keep my hands in that position for the time needed to stabilize the relationship between the vibratory aspect of energy and the will. I must perceive the completion of a flow that accesses the zone circumscribed by the hands. The little finger and thumb are tense so as to guide and contain this flow.

Then I glide from the will to the sides, with the intent of dragging the effect of the quotas of attention and the fine-tuning to the area of unbending intent. The fingers must claw with the fingernails at the lumbar muscles next to the spine and stimulate them. This is another one of the few moments in which we physically touch ourselves.

Then, starting from these muscles, I “scratch” my back and sides below the ribs. I must keep the contact of fingers and nails on the body until I almost get to the navel area; then I launch outward, and I finally lift my arms to strike forward with open hands.

With this movement I pursue different purposes.

The first is to extend as much as possible the fibers related to unbending intent.

This is fundamental. The result of a life led without discipline is that the luminous fibers in this area tangle without purpose. With this gesture, we start extending them, coordinating them with the will in order to allow ourselves to maintain position and direction. This movement also relieves back pain.

If we do this gesture well, a shiver runs up and something gets released in that area.

Another goal, which is the main one in this phase of the sequence, is to increase our available space.

When I strike in front of me with my hands, I apply the intent of weakening the interpretation of the world, making the reflection of the world vibrate until it becomes soft and can be moved a bit farther.

The physical sensation we need to obtain is that the space in which we are moving becomes wider. We could say that, if at the beginning of this part of the sequence we find ourselves obliged to move in a square meter, as we strike and push the interpretation farther, we conquer a much wider area. The area that we create in this way increases the extension of the possible positions of the assemblage point.

This is the space, the extension that I need for stalking, to obtain the environment for the positions that a stalker uses in stalking. This ampler space is the one in which the stalker's dream or the dreamer's extension exist. It is also the space of controlled folly.

After the strike, the hands come down with a serpentine movement whose purpose is to make reality even more elastic. Then they come back to the unbending intent.

As we claw at the muscles at the sides of the vertebral spine, we take two steps back, starting with the left leg, turning clockwise four times in the four directions. Then, we repeat in the four directions, starting with the right leg and turning counterclockwise.

Every time I move, I must look for a very precise sensation.

What happens is that, the moment I strike against my confines, besides weakening the interpretation, I "block" these confines where they are. This means that when I move, instead of following me as usual, my confines stay there where I blocked them.

So, as I move, I take myself to another space and in a new direction, and this expands my available space. This is the sensation we have to feel: our space becomes increasingly expanded, immense compared to the ordinary. Every time I turn I add one more piece, and it is not simply two steps; from the energetic point of view we are adding unimaginable possibilities.

This becomes my "stalking territory."

Every time I turn, the movement must be precise, martial, firm but fluid and flexible. Immediately as I stop I must grasp a gazing area with my perception; but while I transfer my gaze, I must realize that the attention does not only concern the gazing area but is maintained during the movement, too, picking up every detail.

THE NEW ALIGNMENT

The last time I turn (and at that point I am in the initial position, looking at the first gazing area), the right leg goes back, and the left stays extended in the front. The hands come down like before, but they continue descending until they reach the ankle.

From there they come back up the leg that remains extended; I must feel the back of my leg stretching. The function of this is to activate the memories.

Once again, I hitch to the lines of the earth and mix them with the pool of intensity that we have around our feet. I use them to drain the memories, to make sure they radiate, get released from where they are stored.

In this way, also the energy body's memories, the dreamer's memories, start being released.

The left arm goes to the back and comes up, while the right arm is in the front and stays at the level of the vibratory center.

I remain like this, allowing all that I have put so far into motion to accumulate.

The sensation is that everything that has been freed reaches the space between the hands and arms, fills it, assuming a certain order, organizing itself, governed by the vibratory center. It is like feeling a flow of air, a current or fluid rising from below, from the legs, and stabilizing in this area that is limited by the hands and arms until it is filled up.

This is how the totality of the habits would organize the released possibilities. However, I have to obtain a new direction, free of habits, convictions, and personal history.

Therefore, once the space is full, I start bringing my right hand back and the left forward. I do a twist with what I have gathered. It must be a very marked move physically, too, with the back always maintained aligned, straight.

With this twist, I change the direction of the internal alignment; I have a new configuration and have to perceive this organizational change taking place in chain reaction in all the centers as I change my physical condition. All realigns, gets readjusted, finds a new, more flexible organization.

The back stays straight, well aligned.

I turn around 180 degrees and strike again, come down on the right leg in the front, come back up, wind up, and twist again.

In this way, I set off the not-doing of the self.

IGNITING WITH THE EARTH

I release everything, suddenly.

This is the final act of the realignment and guarantees that there are no rational interferences. I relax, turn left 90 degrees and return to the vibratory center. I grab and extend the fibers from the vibratory center.

Now is the moment in which I obtain one of the most important aspects in a warrior's life: the trust in the earth as an aware being.

I abandon my head down to the connection with the earth. I create vortexes with my hands, which are then attracted into the central point. While the hands whirl, the movement must be as soft and natural as possible. Essentially, we have to simply allow the earth's attraction to make the hands move in two swirls, which converge then into the central point where an opening is formed.

When this happens, the hands are attracted into the center as if fitting in a slot. The fingers open, tense, the earth lines stay glued to the fingers, and so we pull them up like strings anchored to the earth. We use these lines to turn on the vibratory center and then the whole body, hitting our chest.

By doing this, the lines of the earth that we have pulled up work like a striker, triggering our self-lighting. We come back down, do it again several times, as much as is needed to obtain this total lighting.

THE CHANGE

The last time we get up, we use the lines of the earth to obtain a new direction, a shift of our attention that is as stable as possible. We try to turn so as to be facing time and succeed in living in real time.

The left arm envelops the chest and hooks onto the head; the right envelops the head directly from behind.

I stay a moment like this to firmly grasp the ordinary direction, then use the hands to turn the head to the left, without touching it, with firmness, determination. Left leg forward, hands open on the time line. Then I reposition myself, come back to standing up straight with a fluid, strong, and precise movement in the initial direction of the sequence, but it is an old-new direction.

THE EFFECT OF SILENCE

We stay still.

We wait as we let ourselves be reached by the cumulative effect of the sequence.

Now, all the inner silence we have accumulated during its execution gathers, layer after layer. We have to be very attentive, especially to the area of the back, the wings of perception, where the layers of silence and heightened attention enter, like breaking waves that overtake our limit and fill us up.

It is the world's silence that reaches us; we have changed time, and thus the world's silence can reach us. Patience is a dam that contains and regulates the flow of silence.

The effects of such inflow organize and express their outcome in the shoulder blades' intensification area, spreading then throughout the body. These layers of silence modify our state and accumulate: the outcome is that, when the fullness of silence is reached, the core of the inner dialogue gets pushed outside.

It floats there, before us.

In that moment, the right perception is "seeing" our mind "flying away."

We are not satisfied with reaching this result; but, applying timing, we grab with our hand this core of the inner dialogue, drag it to the other side as we turn around, and blow it away, dispersing it.

Our breath is connected with infinity because we are now empty (like during the recapitulation), and the inner dialogue is swallowed by infinity that is waiting for us on the other side.

THE SLIDING DOORS

At this point, we reposition ourselves by stepping back with our right foot and slip our hands in the line separating the two sides, with palms facing outward. We open exactly as though we were pushing two sliding doors apart, separating the right and left sides. We create an opening that gives us the special sensation of being divided, activating dreaming and seeing.

Therefore, to further turn on our dreaming and seeing, we stimulate our sides with the fingers, passing them in the spaces between the ribs; we should feel a shiver up our back that starts at the unbending intent as we do it. We stimulate the sides in this way, according to a reiterative rhythm of 4 times: two separate and two close stimulations, to stabilize the heightened attention and make it fully available, exploiting the power of rhythm and repetition in gathering and channeling attention.

GOVERNING SILENCE

Then we hold our hands open, the palms facing each other, at a height just above the will center. The hands must be along the passage of the frontal, lateral flows. The fingers are open and tense, particularly the thumbs and little fingers, so as to coincide with the force of the two lateral flows.

In this phase of the sequence, I am in inner silence; therefore, already facing the second attention; and, to govern it, we need a fully active will. From now on, we try to finalize the silence in order for it to be functional to our abstract purpose and energy body: we accumulate inner silence, layer after layer, until we open this space we keep between our hands.

In order to make it usable, available to the energy body, we have to govern such silence. The silence must grow, rise from the feet and arrive at filling the whole space controlled by the tension in the hands, going up, above the head.

OPENING SILENCE

When this space is saturated, the hands glide along its density, driven and guided by silence itself.

We turn our head to the right, the left hand goes up with the palm looking inwardly; the right hand is down.

We look at the horizon in the direction we have turned to, while with our left hand we materially contain the silence. We have to feel the silence advancing from and toward this horizon that we are looking at, extending its size and then pushing, exerting pressure on the hand and arm that hold it.

Thus, we can direct it to flow and saturate the immense space toward which we are turned.

The open side, the one we are looking at, extends as far as our silence can reach. Then we wait as long as we can as we keep it.

There is an important detail. The side toward which we are looking, that is now on our right, was before on our left, that is the one we had opened as we evoked the rolling force. That is why it turns out to be very easy now to find oneself facing an immensity governed by silence. Moreover, the fact that what was on our left side is now on the right causes a particular and fundamental phenomenon.

Practically, it is as though we were divided in half and then had folded one half over the other, making right and left sides correspond and duplicating ourselves on both sides. As we will see, this is the beginning of a very special maneuver that determines the approach of the energy body: the creation of a temporary double.

THE EXTENSION OF SILENCE

Now our silence is like that of the world; it has mixed and expanded so well that there is no longer a break between the two. When I feel/see this continuity, I insert the right hand into the thickest layer of the inner silence, that is, the internal part of the left hand, without touching it, but slipping the hand into the thickness of silence. This expanded silence stays attached to the hand like glue, and I amplify myself further as I turn 90 degrees to the right. From now on, the gaze is firmly in front of me; it directly looks in the direction that was our left, where I evoked the rolling force and in which I have made the two sides coincide and double. Now my open hands create the confines of a space in which the density of silence increases.

I continue holding this thickness, I feel it pushing my hands and arms outward, but I contain and govern it. When I decide, the right hand, driven and guided by the pressure of silence, descends below the will to connect the control of the second attention and returns out with the palm opened upwardly, supporting the time line. As my hand passes in front of my eyes, I have to continue looking ahead without following the hand with my eyes, but rather carefully picking up the sensation that the hand, as it passes by, hitches to lines from the eyes and pulls them out. Then, as I open the hand, I feel these lines being released along the time line.

In this way, I also free the accumulated silence; it is launched along the time line, obtaining the possibility of total extension. The hand must be kept open exactly in support of this line.

I do the same thing over with the left hand to extend the silence in every direction. The eyes continue looking ahead, toward the open space, and the attention is on the peripheral distance, maintaining the extension.

Therefore, what we have previously accumulated is released along the time line, toward all possible assemblage point positions. We have to feel and intend that, by opening the hand, attention is liberated.

Then I turn the palms down suddenly; I do it to prepare for the final phase of stalking, exploiting the available possibilities with the extension on the time line.

With this sudden turn of the hands to face downward, I modify the state of attention and the quality of the compactness of the emanations inside. I should feel a change in my state, like an enhancement of my lucidity. This change of state is what allows, in the next step, to select the nuclei of the self along the time line.

The kind of compactness I obtain leads us into the suited state of attention.

THE NOT-DOING OF THE SELF

I turn my face to the right; the left hand goes up, maintains and gathers; the right hand goes down. I let all that comes from the time line accumulate and implement the not-doing of the self, the final phase of stalking, by performing a very special form of recapitulation.

In short, what I try to obtain in this moment is the interruption of my ordinary continuity. This is essential; without it, it is impossible to reach the predominance of the energy body. The principle is that we have to be stopped, and the best way is for us to understand the need to stop ourselves and do it voluntarily and consciously.

The only true instrument that can make us reach such result is the recapitulation, which must be done constantly, in a continuous and systematic way. Thus, I want to state beforehand that, in order to implement this and other parts of the sequence, it is essential to practice the recapitulation, too. Having clarified this point, we can see how the movement of the not-doing of the self acts.

While I am turned to the right, I look directly into the time line, and the first things I encounter are the obstacles, the guardians that prevent me from moving to other positions. The nuclei of the self, those hard kerns that gather and maintain my characteristics; the inventory of myself.

Perceptually, it is like a rope with knots that flows toward us. These knots are filtered and stopped by the hand; and they are precisely the obstacles we are looking for.

As soon as I get one, I breathe in, like in the classical recapitulation, starting on the right shoulder and turning the head toward the left shoulder; then I breathe out bringing the head back to the right shoulder. I do it three times.

The first sweeping breath is done with the right hand down and the left up to the side. In the second, I move the left hand edgeways to a point between the eyes, do a sweeping breath and cross my eyes as they sweep by the hand and look at it. In the third breath, the right hand goes over the vibratory center, the left hand stays edgeways in front of the face, and at the moment of breathing out both hands turn and push outward. During these three respirations we recapitulate ourselves.

Once we learn to do the sequence really well, we truly succeed in freeing ourselves of real blocks, sets of convictions about the world, lines of intent that we had even activated at very remote times.

The principle is that we recapitulate what the time line brings us. We have to wait, before beginning the first inhalation, for something to arrive from that open distance, something that concerns us.

Consider that in this moment the time line is open, everything is totally available and fluid, including the founding traits of our image of the world and of ourselves. The characteristic of our human form and the intents enacted by us during our existence are fluctuating, available to our will. By connecting breathing, eyes, and will, we can select the main cores and push them into infinity, which is there in front of us, open, where they get devoured.

The recapitulation can take on various overtones. The most abstract one consists in using the extension of the time line. It is a mode that directly deprives the human form of structure.

Remember that the eyes are unhooked from the mind and hooked to the will; so what arrives has been reached and brought by the will itself.

This type of recapitulation can be done as an act in itself; yet, before doing it, it is necessary to open the time line.

THE AVAILABILITY OF INTENT

After having pushed away our continuity core, the hands come back and the face looks ahead again. The left hand is open before the face and the right is on the vibratory center, both with palms facing outward. We look through the hand, between the middle and ring fingers; in this way, we are hidden, waiting. The left eye is covered, while the right looks through the opening.

We have to intend being at a threshold, that passage between the worlds; between the world of limitedness and that of the availability of intent, which is just beyond the passage between the fingers.

We have to stake our whole availability, that is, be ready to wait even forever and be ready to be included into infinity without regrets or doubts, completely trusting our total energy.

From this privileged position, we evoke intent, make pressure on the world with our heightened attention and wait for the moment in which it turns to us. The world is not idle; it reacts to real stimulation, and particularly reacts to the attention.

When it happens, it is as though the world turned, not the usual world, but the world as the will of infinity, as the rule over the emanations. In other words, the active side of infinity turns its attention to us. It is the world made of awareness. Everything becomes alive, intense, luminous.

Staying there, behind the hands, puts us in the position of the stalker with respect to intent. We send the message that we are stalking, available. This is the moment in which we harmonize, in which we coordinate stalking and intent. In the exact instant in which there is attention and action in the world, that is, when the active side of infinity responds, we feel or see intensity landing on our hands. So we gather the type of attention that is released, the outcome of the ever active alignment (that is, intent), and we push it inside our eyes, because intent is evoked with the eyes that we thus make alive with respect to it.

After having inserted this new capability into our eyes, we extend it along the time line, opening the arms, palms up. Thus we extend the possibility of evoking intent to all of the time modes.

I must clearly feel that I insert into the eyes and then extract from the eyes what I have grabbed in front of me; it is a physical sensation. What has been freed in front of me is a type of attention that is incredibly intense and authentic, impersonal, non-human, non-animal, non-vegetal, non-inorganic. It is the active side of infinity's attention; we capture and insert it into our eyes, changing their luminosity.

When we extend along the time line and then open the hands, the totality of all possibilities goes through us, uniting us to infinity in every direction starting from the will. The connection between the will, eyes, and time line must be very clear. We hold and sustain this moment.

Now I turn to the right (clockwise), inverting the hands. Every time I turn, the hand corresponding to the foot on which I rotate goes on top. I change hand and change the eye that is looking through the space between the fingers.

I turn three times.

THE TIME OF INFINITY

The last time I will find myself with my right hand on top (therefore, I will have turned on the right foot) and the left in front of the vibratory center. I use this hand as a pivot around which both hands rotate; the hand that was in front of the eyes goes to the will and the other rotates and stays there, the palm now facing the vibratory center.

I extend thus this balance between stalking and intent to the area of the will: while maintaining the stability of the vibratory center, I transfer the balance onto the second attention.

I fine-tune these two centers as though I were turning knobs, until I feel a clear, physical wellbeing, something getting in place.

I shift and push down along the sides, dreaming and seeing, to transport the fine-tuning down, all the way. At the level of the two lower intensification points I gather, tie together, and then I come back up to push all of this precision into my eyes, balancing dreaming and seeing with the ability to evoke intent with the eyes.

Now I adjust all of the other points, first by sliding briefly over the time line and then by descending with palms facing down over the two upper intensification points. I continue sliding to the center for decisions, then to the vibratory center, the will, and finally to the area of unbending intent.

I thus fine-tune all the centers on the balance between stalking and intent. The purpose is to feel that I am adjusting every center; but I have to perceive beforehand the passage near the centers. In other words, for instance, before starting coming down toward the upper intensification points, I have to already feel the effect of the insertion of these lines of intensity into the centers. Before heading toward the center for decisions, when I am still under the collarbones and am just intending to move, I am already reached by the effect obtained at the base of the throat; and before I move toward the vibratory center, when I am still on the center for decisions I already feel with clarity the action on the vibratory center; and so on.

The detail about anticipation is essential. I am apparently early with respect to the sensations I should feel. Actually, what happens is that we are fine-tuning on the time of infinity, on the real time, deprived of the lateness due to the interpretation process. So, the point is not that we are feeling early, but that we are feeling what is already happening at that moment.

The true matter is that we are usually late because of our interpretation process; now, however, we are in the real time, at least with our ability to feel, and thus we are faster.

If this happens, it means that the energy body is already present.

THE CONTROL ON THE SECOND ATTENTION

I end up on the area of unbending intent. From here, I claw (without touching the body), hold, and extend forward as I squat down, involving the will during the movement. I must make sure that the will is channeled and pushed through the layers of the earth, the alignments contained by the earth.

The arms do not rest on the knees but stay slightly lifted in order to create the right tension and attention.

I keep this position long enough for a complete "bubble" to gather, until I feel I have obtained the fullness of the area in front of me, where the control on the second attention has now gathered. At that point, I start moving the arms with open hands, literally resting them on this area of greater intensity. I have to create a stable flow as a supporting base.

I stay latched onto this area and extend, increase, intensify it; I use it precisely to support myself on it. In this way, I can use the control over the second attention to push myself up, to bring this control area to the totality of myself.

COINCIDING WITH INTENT

The hands come up on top of the two lateral flows, where they are grafted into the time line; then they push downward all the way to the area of the sartorius muscles. We support ourselves on the area of greater density that we have made before and, as the hands push, we get up on this push. The sensation that we are supporting ourselves on a denser core must be clear.

The hands stay down, then they come up and down again along the two lateral flows, to the intensification points.

It is a fundamental moment: with this thrust downward, I cancel, at least temporarily, everything that can interfere with the predominance of the energy body: thus, inner dialogue, human form, convictions, habits, etcetera.

I empty myself completely. Not simply empty, I am like intent, I practically created a space that immediately called upon intent, which was there, ready thanks to the preceding maneuvers. Intent is pressing and, as soon as one removes what opposes resistance, it arrives and fills up every available space.

With this gesture, I obtain the coincidence with intent; for a moment I am neither myself nor a human being; I am both things beyond what they would be. I keep my identity before infinity, but I do not carry anything with me of what I usually drag along.

I am brand new and made of intent.

THE PERCEPTION OF THE DREAMER

Face turned to the right, right hand clawing on the opposite side above the left collarbone's intensification point and at eye level, on the time line. I do again a special form of recapitulation.

Breathing in, I turn my head to the left; as the hand passes before the eyes, the fingers hook onto and extract the eyes' fibers connected to the time line, then the hand pauses a moment on the other intensification point on the right.

At this point, the inhalation finishes and I am holding my breath.

I start breathing out as the head stays still and the hand proceeds along the time line, continuing to extract and extend the fibers from the eyes to their complete extension. Now I open my hand, slowly, toward infinity. I must feel that the perception and intensity connected to the will are released, without limits. It is a physical sensation, like having fibers uncoiling from the will and, passing inside the body and through the eyes, continuing along the hand toward infinity.

This respiration is really carried out along the time line. We use the intent of the recapitulation to shift to a completely new time mode that facilitates the predominance of the energy body.

What lies in the direction beyond the hand is also on the opposite side, on the side I am looking at, because time is cyclical.

And so, as I look down the time line, I see myself looking at myself.

This is the dreamer's look.

It is the first moment we notice the presence of the dreamer.

I repeat it all starting from the left side. This special application of the recapitulation, as I was saying, can move us on the time line; thus, we exploit the recapitulation's characteristics to remove ourselves from the usual time mode; that is, we directly recapitulate the habitual position of the assemblage point.

This allows to perceive the dreamer's presence along the time line that is located into another time mode. That is how I can see it while it sees me.

RELEASING THE DREAMER'S MEMORIES

I left the right hand edgewise above the intensification point located below the right collarbone, but at the level of the time line.

With my right hand, I push the right side into the left. In order to do it, I exploit the elasticity of the time line; the sensation is of moving and inserting from one eye to the other and then from one side to the other, something that presses against the hand, something with solidity and dimension, like inserting a telescopic pipe from one eye to the other.

The hand passes in front of the face, stops above the upper left intensification point, turns downward and then comes down at an oblique angle. This oblique trajectory must pass between the vibratory center and the will. Then, I reach the right knee and stimulate it in a particular way.

What I am trying to obtain is to release the dreamer's memories, which are beyond our ordinary life, which are on a parallel line. By pushing the right side into the left, I cancel every residual interference and modify the current alignment, the precise attitude of the time mode. I drag this special mix with the oblique movement that mixes the fibers in a way that is not conform to the normal perceptual coercion, and I bring it to the knee.

The knees are related to every kind of memories but, in this case, the type of attention we exert is aimed at releasing the dreamer's memories.

I have to give up control definitely, allow the emanations that make me up, the memory of myself as a sensation to guide my precise movements.

There are exact points in the knee that, if stimulated in the correct way, release the dreamer's memories. These points and the way of stimulating them change continuously; therefore, there is no repeatable procedure. Essentially, I have to be extremely sensitive and allow the body to act on its own. The pressure must not last too long or too little. There are precise points, but they are not always the same; and also the duration and intensity of the pressure change from time to time.

The way in which the hand acts is guided by the energy body's will. I realize that I have stimulated the knee correctly because, in this case, when I get up again, my perception is changed. What has been freed reaches us, modifying our state; even just a little, but the change must take place in a very clear way. It is not a matter of searching it in this case, but of allowing it to come.

It is a variation of our state of awareness and perception.

I repeat the whole process on the other side.

THE COINCIDENCE OF ATTENTION

In the areas of the Sartorius muscles, near the lower intensification points, I latch onto what has been released from the legs. Now my intent is to connect the earth lines, my fibers with enhanced intensity, and the memory of the energy body; I use this connection to create an indentation in the luminous egg that allows to make all the layers coincide up to the physical body.

I do it in a very specific point. However, I have to look for this exact point within a certain area that can be found by extending the arms almost completely, generally a little above the navel, shifted 10-15 centimeters to the right.

In the physical body, it usually corresponds to a point just below our ribcage or right where it starts. It must be our right sensation to act as a guide, but it corresponds to the area where we previously formed the indentation to hook onto the rolling force, which is not exactly the point where we were keeping our fingers, on our ribcage, but a bit further ahead, a little more to the front.

To find this point, first of all you have to find the limit of the luminous egg; you should be able to feel the distance where, as you push toward yourself, you can immediately feel some physical correspondence, a special sensitivity that is transmitted from that distance as though you were touching your body. That is the right distance. At this distance and in connection with the area I indicated, you have to find a point where, as you push inwardly, a change in your state of attention takes place.

As I was saying, what we intend to do is to push from the confines of the luminous egg in order to create an indentation that arrives at the right side on the physical body. The effective sensation is that, as we push on the right side from a distance, it is as though we were touching ourselves physically. I use this sensation to make the attention of the energy body coincide with the attention of the physical body.

This is the way in which I completely activate the second attention. The notch I create, this indentation, is an actual space or housing for the second attention.

From the energetic point of view, I am bringing the luminous egg's layers closer to one another.

THE TEMPORARY DOUBLE

Now I put my right hand in front of the right eye and claw; the left hand is in front of the sartorius muscle. I must create a temporary double, a copy of my centers and intensification points on an axis that is a step away from me, sideways, within the limits of my peripheral vision.

This is an important detail: I must perform all the movements within the limits of my peripheral vision but not outside of it. The perception of what I do with my hand when I extend it must be a mix of seeing and feeling, but clearly perceivable.

Thus, I extract the fibers from the right eye, control, and extend them along the time line to a position that is at a distance from me that corresponds to my limit as a human being: at the threshold.

I settle them there and stabilize this new position. I must really wedge, insert them, find the right placement that already exists in that exact point. Also in this case, I let myself be guided by the will and by the sensations and perceptions it evokes.

When I have inserted every fiber in the right place, the will and the body relax; they do it every time I perform the right movement.

Here, it is essential to intend the precision in creating this copy of myself.

Then I come down, return to the body and do the same thing with the center for decisions and the right, upper intensification point. I come down again, move over the will to maintain control over the second attention, and repeat the operation with the vibratory center and the upper part of the right side. I come down further and shift the will, the lower part of the right side, and the unbending intent. Finally, I hook onto the intensification point of the sartorius muscle, place it on the double's axis, and use it as a firm point to spin around, remaining in the exact, same position.

I repeat the whole procedure on the left side to complete the temporary double.

COINCIDING WITH THE DOUBLE

At the end, I grab the point on the sartorius of the left side that I have just shifted and use it to pull myself to the side. With a skip to the left, I make myself coincide with the axis of the temporary double, while with my left arm I close the preceding position, which is the ordinary, dreaming position, what we call reality. Now, I have to wait for the double and temporary centers to coincide with the dreamer's original copy, that is, myself. I wait until I feel that they have settled in, one after the other; they click into place, coincide along my body.

I have to incorporate the copy, to include it.

THE TWIN POSITION

When this takes place, the moment this coincidence between physical body and temporary double occurs, it means that I have moved with my physical body into a twin position, a voluntary, dreaming position.

I have moved along the time line in a total form.

I do not make a real double, but shift to another position; I have the traits of a double, but with the totality of myself: also with my physical body. Transferring myself in this manner into an alternative dreaming position attracts the energy body irresistibly; it draws it nearer, a step away to the right with respect to the point where I was before.

THE PREDOMINANCE OF THE ENERGY BODY

I turn to the right, toward the point where I was before, and should have a very strange surprise. In front of me, I now perceive someone's presence.

So I wait for this presence to become denser, until I am attracted; at that precise moment, I step forward to coincide with my energy body.

Then I let myself be pulled toward it.

It is like finding oneself in front of a mirror, and the image in the mirror steps forward as I do, too, ending up coinciding with the exact point where the sequence began. There is a correspondence between action and intent, a mirror-like, simultaneous movement that makes us graft into this being.

Then, I turn to the initial direction and am in the ordinary dreaming position with the predominance of the energy body.

I am thus in the stalker's dream and also in the extension of the dreamer.

At the end of the sequence, I have to find myself with my feet in the exact, initial position.

BREATHING

The respiration during the sequence alternates moments in which the breathing is free with others of the utmost control. It is not easy to describe it with due precision, because in almost all movements inhalations and exhalations are modulated.

This means that, guided by the will, they vary in intensity as they are done, so as to intend and accompany both movements and sensations.

As a general rule, try to have the necessary abandonment and control to make sure that the intensity of the breathing adapts to the movement and sensations and sustains them. This translates into the fact that inhalations and exhalations have a non-linear pace.

In other words, the amount of air you breathe in or out varies; it rises and drops, accelerates, slows down; it accompanies the physical act, the attention, and the perception. It accompanies every type of variation, including deviations in the time mode.

Moreover, the duration of the sequence can vary each time, and this obviously affects the way we breathe.

In any case, keep in mind that, in every passage of the sequence, you can introduce one or more free respirations if you have need for more time between one movement and the other, to wait for its effects to play out.

Furthermore, my advice is to worry about the breathing only after you will have acquired the movements and related sensations with precision. Thus, in the first phase, breathe freely, except for the points where, in the preceding description of the movements, I give clear indications about the breathing.

The right sensations are the essential aspect: focus on those above all.

At any rate, to be able to coordinate sensations and breathing, there is an unfailing method: connecting the way we breathe to the sensations evoked by the movements.

This means that it must be the sensations that lead the intensity of the breathing.

That is what I mean when I talk about modulated inhalations and exhalations. On the other hand, it can also work the opposite way: modulating the breathing guides and makes the right sensations more easily perceivable.

We always breathe in and out through the nose, never through our mouth, unless otherwise specified. Breathing through the mouth disperses energy.

THE EARTH

The respiration is free until we are about to close our hands above our head. As the hands cover the last tract, we have to breathe in slowly and deeply. Therefore, the moment in which this inspiration starts will depend on our capacity for control over the depth of our inhalation. As we progress, it will always start earlier.

We breathe out as we come down frontally, reaching the area of the will.

THE DIRECTION

A single, energetic and deep inhalation is taken as the hands are brought to the vibratory center. Then we exhale and use this exhalation to accompany the flow of the vibratory center. The exhalation is controlled and its intensity is constant, in order to maintain uniformity, continuity in the flow's current. You have to govern it from the will.

THE CHANGE OF INTENSITY

We breathe in very deeply as we lift our arms. We hold, stabilizing the gazing zone and, once it is stabilized, we breathe our inner dialogue out with a long, uniform, and controlled exhalation through the window.

We use the exhalation to empty our mind.

THE ATTENTION BEYOND THE LIMITS

Breathing in, we expand our attention; the arms and hands open. It is as though the arms were widened by the inhalation. The chest opens, and the shoulder blades close.

Remember that you can introduce free breathing at any time, as long as you begin the next movement with the right breathing phase.

Therefore, in this moment, for instance, as the hands are resting on the time line, you can very well wait for the right sensation.

Never rush into a forced breathing pattern; the right sensations are a great deal more important. For the same reason, do not lose your focus on the body in order to follow the directions on breathing described here. Rather, breathe freely.

THE SENSITIVITY OF THE VIBRATORY CENTER

I exhale with continuity as I come down toward the vibratory center.

I inhale, going back up with the hands toward the two peripheral areas, a very deep, regular breath. Also in this case does the inhalation help us spread out our arms, the chest opens, the shoulder blades close. I hold my breath as I look for the intensity beyond the limits. Then I have to exhale during the whole time when I move the fingers and come down along the extended fibers. Therefore, it must be a very slow and controlled exhalation, to prevent the lack of air from rushing me.

Rather, as you move your fingers up high breathe freely and then exhale only as you come down.

The exhalation must also be modulated according to the movements of hands and fingers.

THE DISCIPLINE OF ACTIONS

I breathe in throughout the way.

PATIENCE

I continue the inhalation that I started coming up to the center for decisions and continue it until my hands are at my sides. So, it must be very slow and controlled, deep, complete and modulated, in order to define the different moments along the course.

We breathe out the moment the hands are positioned by our sides: a slow and controlled exhalation, connected with the sensation that the tie between the will and the area of unbending intent is being consolidated.

THE PREPARATION

I breathe in, still with my hands by the sides and then, when I start going down, I breathe out.

I breathe in coming back up and then breathe out again, once I have reached the "lifebuoy." I can breathe freely every time the hands stay at the sides, if I need more time to gather the right sensations.

CALLING THE WORLD FORTH

I breathe in as I lift the hands and breathe out the moment they turn outwardly.

As a rule, every time in the sequence we align with the world, we breathe out.

Inhalation and exhalation are rather fast, just as the movement is, but not shallow. Every single breath must reach the will.

RECEIVING THE WORLD

Breathe in as the hands circle downward and upward; then breathe out again when the arms extend toward the world.

THE DISCIPLINE OF UNBENDING INTENT

We breathe in as our arms lift and breathe out as they go toward the vibratory center. Then the breathing is repeated like in the previous step: inhaling as we go up, exhaling as we come down to the vibratory center, inhaling throughout the way to the sides, exhaling-inhaling, and again exhaling as we go down, inhaling coming back up, breathing out at the sides.

INNER STRENGTH

Breathing in as the hands are lifted. We exhale and then breathe freely as we modulate the flow of the vibratory center.

I breathe in as I draw my hands closer to the vibratory center, I attract it with my inhalation. Free respiration as the flow is concentrated.

CONTROL

I breathe out as I push on the will, so I must have reached the right condition to push the nucleus of intensity into the will, coinciding with the end of an inhalation. This coincidence may not occur the first times. It does not matter; in time, it will take place spontaneously.

There are many passages in the sequence in which it is necessary to learn to end free breathing in the right way, to coincide with the continuation of the sequence (having inhaled or exhaled at the right moment).

THE INFALLIBLE GUIDE

I breathe in, extending the will's fibers. I exhale and then I breathe freely (if I need more time) as I connect them to the earth.

I inhale as my hands go toward the hips; I exhale when I extend them toward the world.

I repeat the same pattern: breathing in as I extend, breathing out as I latch on, inhaling going toward the hips, and exhaling turning on to the world.

Then I repeat again: breathing in as I extend and exhaling when I push on the sides. The latter exhalation must be extremely controlled and modulated. It accompanies the pressure that we exert and it is consciously used to enhance its effect. So it must be modulated in the sense that in the movements in which the push is more delicate the exhalation will be lighter, and vice versa.

We should start realizing that our breathing is part of intending.

This principle becomes very clear through the practice of the recapitulation.

THE REALIGNMENT

I inhale as the hands come up along the sides and extend forward. Exhale as they position themselves and then breathe freely while modulating the flow of the vibratory center.

As I come closer to the vibratory center with my hands, I breathe in. I breathe freely while the flow is concentrated.

I inhale grabbing this intensity and while I extend it; then I exhale as I turn it onto the world. I breathe in as I grab and pull back, and then exhale when I drag on to the will.

EXTENDING UNBENDING INTENT

Breathing freely as I handle the will, I inhale when the hands glide over the sides and continue inhaling until I grab the area of the unbending intent. I hold my breath and then begin exhaling from the point where I start extending the fibers toward the world, that is, more or less from the moment the hands move past the waist. The inhalation or exhalation must be modulated, that is, accompany and adapt to the variation of the movement's intensity.

Every time I come back and slide toward the area of unbending intent, I start breathing in; and every time I extend toward the world, I breathe out. Finally, with a last inhalation, I reach the center for decisions.

The inhalation becomes longer each time.

THE OPENING

Once I have reached the center for decisions, I breathe out the moment I latch onto it and then I start inhaling as I separate the right from the left side. This inhalation is modulated in two movements. When I get to the two intensification points, I turn my hands outwardly, and this marks a change in the intensity of the breathing.

I breathe out as the hands come in front of the eyes.

THE LINES OF FORCE

While my hands move over my head and reach the fibers of the shoulder blades, I breathe in.

I breathe out and then breathe freely as I look for the fibers of the wings of perception.

Again, I breathe in as the hands come back over the head and then, going down the vertical flows, I keep breathing freely, if necessary, after a long, controlled and modulated exhalation. In other words, I use the exhalation going down as far as I can, as long as I have sufficient air. Ideally, one should go the whole way with a single exhalation. However, if the search for the right sensations requires more time, the air you have will not suffice. Therefore, like always, the right sensations take precedence.

THE CHANGE IN DIRECTION

I breathe in, lifting the unit of intent, and breathe out grabbing the center for decisions.

Like before, I do a modulated inhalation while I separate the right from the left side.

As I do the change in direction, I breathe out: the head to the right, right hand on the will area, protecting, the left hand up, with the palm edgewise facing out.

OPENING THE LEFT SIDE

I breathe in as I change position and insert the hand into the natural weld, hold for a moment, and then start breathing out while the hand goes down.

The inhalation must be very deep, so as to have sufficient air to accompany the hand's descent.

As I have already mentioned, the (modulated) exhalation we do as the hand comes down helps guiding the hand as it slides down naturally, relaxed, and finding the right path.

We breathe in when we enter underneath the layers of the luminous egg and extend the fibers: deep and modulated inhalation. We repeat until the sensation of opening becomes clear.

Then, when we reverse the direction in which we operate, the breathing works the other way around: we breathe in as the hand is lifted by the updraft, and we breathe out as we enter underneath the layers. The updraft is strictly related to the inhalation.

All of these breathing cycles should be modulated, varying the intensity of the breath according to the variations we perceive in the left side and on the way down and up along the natural weld.

THE GAZE BEYOND INTERPRETATION

We continue the last inhalation as we raise the hand. It ends when we put our hand in front of the left eye. Holding our breath, we turn and exhale while the arm is extended. The exhalation is continued beyond the moment when the arm is completely extended, because it must be the breath that guides the perception toward that distance beyond what is conceivable and is not in the ordinary time.

Consequently, the inhalation must be very deep, since the exhalation will have to sustain the attention as long as needed. This exhalation will also have to be modulated: more intense initially, then increasingly light and controlled, as though it were moving away toward that infinite distance until it disappears.

EXPANDING THE LEFT SIDE

I breathe in as soon as I turn and face forward and bring my hand at the level of the left eye, grabbing the fibers that issue from the relationship between the eyes and the time line. I continue breathing in as I start extending them and begin breathing out more or less when the hand goes beyond the upper intensification point.

The way we do this exhalation is essential; we will call it the "exhalation along the time line" and we will find it again at other times later on, during the sequence.

Once we have succeeded in fine-tuning it, this exhalation acts as a guide for the respiration during the whole sequence; in other words, it allows to sense how to connect breathing, sensations, movements, and assemblage point position.

During this exhalation it is necessary to tie very precisely the exhalation itself with the sensations that issue from the will. The moment we grab the fibers from the left eye and start extending them, we should realize that these fibers originate from the area of the will. They have continuity: they issue from the area of the will, go through the whole body and extend out of the eye as we pull them. This extension is connected to the exhalation, especially in the final phase.

When the arm is completely spread out and the hand opens, the breath, thus connected, allows this extension of the fibers not to stop and continue without end along the time line. The sensation is that the breath continues extracting the fibers from the area of the will, through the eye, and then toward this infinite line.

It is very pleasant for the will.

I repeat the same breathing pattern in all of the four extensions, and in all four we prolong the extension on the left side.

The respiration along the time line has the same nature as the sweeping breath used in the recapitulation. Learning to perform well the breathing along the time line is essential in order to activate the intent of the recapitulation.

We will see it better in the sections of the sequence relevant to the recapitulation.

THE PROTECTED STANCE

I breathe in as I place the hand on the time line and breathe out as I step back.

THE ROLLING FORCE – Preparation

I breathe in as I rotate and position myself to face the rolling force.

While I wait for the arrival of the rolling force, I hold my breath or breathe freely, depending on the time needed to perceive its charge. It is important to be full of air at the moment in which the hands snap forward.

The following exhalation is very controlled and divided in three phases. First, a short but intense exhalation, concentrated and strong, when the left hand expands the space. This one is followed by another equal exhalation when the right hand moves to anticipate the movement of the rolling force. The two exhalations are separated by a very brief moment, an instant in which we hold our breath. This moment serves to mark the time and control over the aspects of the rolling force. Then the exhalation is ended as the right hand traces the inward spiral, but only for as long as it is outside the limit defined by the left hand.

The moment the right hand is inside such limit, we start the new inhalation that ends when the right hand is inserted in the ribcage.

This breathing is repeated in all the cycles.

THE ROLLING FORCE – Harmonization

As we wait for the perceptual contact with the rolling force, we breathe out. If it is necessary to wait longer, we can breathe freely.

When we start to latch onto the movement of the rolling force, we begin the inhalation, which must be very controlled, stable, deep. The breathing continues freely, but always with very uniform and deep inhalations and exhalations.

However, when the arms align we have to be inhaling.

NOT INDULGING

We turn as we breathe in and breathe out as soon as we are stable and our eyes cross as they look at the hand placed edgewise.

THE MANEUVERABILITY OF THE VIBRATORY ASPECT

I make a deep and strong inhalation while the two hands pass one above and one below the vibratory center. Then a slow and modulated exhalation ensues, accompanying the eye movement.

The inhalation is very deep, continuous and complete. When it is over, we hold the breath for a moment, settling the breath in the center for decisions. The sensation is similar to swallowing.

The exhalation must be extremely controlled to allow sustaining the continuity of the gaze (along both diagonals), modulating it according to the intensity of the attention, and directing the will, disciplining it.

This exhalation must be almost imperceptible; indeed, in time it will become completely imperceptible.

The same procedure is repeated by inverting the hands. During the last movement, the gaze, led by the exhalation, slides along the diagonals and then also horizontally.

As mentioned, the described way of breathing forms the control of the new directions, while the way of using the eyes allows us to find these new directions, examining the details of the world with continuity. The harmonization of these two elements (breathing and gazing) produces in time a special “sensitivity to intent” and also to what the Toltecs call the “escape nooks.”

The sensitivity to intent allows warriors to use their eyes and breathing to evoke intent, relate to it, and act in tune with it.

OPENING THE TIME LINE

We start breathing in as we put our opposing hands one above and one below, and we continue as we lift the hands to grab the wings of perception.

I exhale and then breathe freely while I look for and grab the fibers of the wings of perception.

I breathe in going over the head again and then breathe out as I drop the fibers in the two lateral flows; we use the exhalation to accompany the descent.

Breathe freely, gazing at the horizon. Then I breathe out as I extend my arms until the hands reach the farthest point in front of me, and I breathe in when I widen and expand the horizon on both sides.

The breathing is free as I wait for the change in perception, observing the horizon.

We try to connect breathing and will.

THE TIME NICHE

I breathe in going down, breathe out, and if necessary I breathe freely, as I catch the details.

I inhale as I come up and down again and, once more, I breathe out as I catch the details.

TIMING OR THE STALKER'S HARMONY

I inhale deeply as I get up and then do a very slow and controlled exhalation while I am positioned, waiting for the attention quotas.

If the signal arrives during the exhalation, as we go down with our hand toward the area of the peripheral vision, we do a quick, concentrated intake of air. If not, we breathe freely as we wait and then we do this concentrated inhalation as we go down.

We breathe out as we grab the availability of attention, breathe in rising diagonally with our hand, exhale while we distribute on the right side. Now, as we distribute the attention quota on the centers, we should do a very controlled inhalation. It should be modulated by the centers themselves, as though the hand were controlled by the breathing, which is in turn controlled by the centers.

We breathe out as we position ourselves again and repeat the same breathing pattern on the other side.

THE PRINCIPLES OF STALKING

I continue the last inhalation (the one tied to the distribution on the centers) until the left hand goes down, grabs and starts pressing on the sartorius muscle.

At that moment we begin breathing out, slowly. This exhalation must accompany the attention down to the peripheral areas. We breathe freely if we need time until the moment I start with the hands. I breathe in as I go to grab and exhale while I take the attention quotas.

I breathe in coming up the sides, breathe out pushing into the earth.

Breathing in as I tie to the earth.

Half, rapid and energetic exhalation as I come back upwards.

THE QUOTAS OF ATTENTION

I finish the controlled exhalation, going down toward the wings of perception. I breathe freely if I need more time to look with care for the fibers that I should grasp.

I inhale as I come over the head.

I breathe out, releasing the fibers in the two lateral flows to accompany their descent.

The breathing is free, as I wait along the time line.

I do a strong, fast, and deep inhalation while I reach the attention quotas on the time line. I breathe out as I clasp them, inhale as I reach the center for decisions, and then breathe out while the attention quota is being absorbed.

I breathe freely while I wait, breathe in quickly and deeply when I shoot out to grasp, breathe out while grabbing, inhale as I drag on to the vibratory center, and then exhale while the whole gets absorbed.

THE FINE-TUNING

A single inhalation: deep, modulated, extremely controlled.

THE SPACE FOR THE NEW POSITIONS

I breathe out as the hands move toward the unbending intent.

As I reach and grasp the area of unbending intent, I inhale.

Now I exhale in two stages. The first part of this exhalation is strong, clear-cut; it accompanies the blow given by the hands on the confines of the luminous egg.

The second is very modulated and controlled; it accompanies the serpentine movement. It must be just as flexible. Obviously, the first part of the exhalation must leave enough air for the second.

I breathe in deeply again as I return with my hands to the area of unbending intent and turn 90 degrees.

This breathing pattern is repeated in the four directions, clockwise and counter-clockwise.

THE NEW ALIGNMENT

The last time I turn, the exhalation accompanies the hands that go down to the ankle.

Then I do a single, deep inhalation while I come back up along the leg and to the back, until I reposition myself. Also this inhalation must be modulated, according to the different moments of the passage.

Once I have positioned myself, I exhale with extreme control, using this exhalation to favor the rise of new possibilities into the space that I create with my hands.

If I need to wait any longer, I breathe freely.

Then, as I twist the upper body, I breathe in until the left hand reaches more or less the left shoulder. From that moment on, I breathe out as the new, inner alignment settles in.

I breathe in deeply as I turn 180 degrees and repeat the same breathing pattern as before.

IGNITING WITH THE EARTH

As I turn, I refrain from breathing, and I inhale as I extend the fibers of the vibratory center.

I breathe out, abandoning myself to the earth. However, also this exhalation must have a good degree of control. I do not empty myself completely as I go down, because the inhalation continues as I create the two whirls. It must vary, thus modulate, in the two phases.

After that, I do a long inhalation that helps me extracting the lines from the earth and igniting the vibratory center. Then I breathe out as I go back down again.

We repeat this way every time we go down and back up.

THE CHANGE

The last time we get back up we inhale until we position our arms around the head. Then we hold our breath as we prepare to gather the right attention.

We exhale completely as we turn to the left.

We breathe in again, holding our hands open on the time line and finish this inhalation as we are already moving forward with our right leg.

Then we reposition ourselves breathing out. The way we do this exhalation is very important, because this is the key moment in the sequence.

It must be extremely controlled, extended and modulated with continuity to allow me to accompany the arrival of the intensity levels. The degree of discipline that we can develop, expressing it in the exhalation and descent of the arms, is essential for the further developments of the sequence.

The will is completely spread out.

THE EFFECT OF SILENCE

We breathe freely as we stay still and enjoy the cumulative effect of the sequence.

We inhale in two phases as we grab the nucleus of the internal dialogue: the first part is short, clear-cut, precise; and then we breathe in deeply as we turn around.

Then, we blow away this nucleus of the internal dialogue by using the exhalation from the mouth for the first and only time during the whole sequence.

THE SLIDING DOORS

We stay empty while we reposition ourselves and then we do an inhalation in two phases as we insert our hands into the separation line and open the sliding doors.
There is a modulated exhalation during the reiterative stimulations on the sides.

GOVERNING SILENCE

The exhalation continues, with the last phase (the fifth) when we position correctly the hands in the lateral flows.
We breathe freely as we accumulate inner silence.

OPENING SILENCE

When the hands slide along the density of silence and the head turns, we do a very deep inhalation, followed by an exhalation that we use to intend the horizon of silence.
We breathe freely as we sustain the silence.

THE EXTENSION OF SILENCE

I do a very deep inhalation when I turn, followed by an exhalation to intend the horizon of silence. Then I breathe freely while the density of silence increases.

A deep inhalation takes place when the hand moves down below the will and rises up again.

As soon as the hand starts positioning itself, opening, I breathe out along the time line as described above. So I release the fibers of the will along the time line itself. I repeat with the left hand.

I breathe in briefly when the palms quickly turn downward and then breathe out holding this position.

THE NOT-DOING OF THE SELF

I breathe in deeply when I turn, exhale to summon the keepers of the confines of the self, and breathe freely as I wait for them coming.

Then I use the sweeping breath of the recapitulation in the subsequent phase. Thus, I breathe in when the head turns toward the left shoulder and breathe out when it turns toward the right.

Remember that also the sweeping breath is a breath along the time line. With the inhalation we gather the memories, with the exhalation we disperse them.

With the last exhalation we free ourselves of the nucleus of continuity, then we breathe in as we bring our hands close to the face.

THE AVAILABILITY OF INTENT

The breathing is free as we look through the fingers and evoke intent; yet, it is closely tied to the ability and possibility of doing it. Therefore, it is not casual, but endowed with great discipline and connected to the will.

From the moment when the hands move to gather the attention of the world, we start a very controlled and modulated inhalation that must last until we have pushed everything we gathered inside our eyes.

As we open our arms, from the moment the hands start moving away from the eyes we do an exhalation along the time line that must last as much as possible, be extremely controlled and extended.

We breathe in as we turn, breathe out as soon as we are positioned.

We repeat every time we turn.

THE TIME OF INFINITY

I breathe in as I rotate the hands, bringing them over the will and the vibratory center.

As I breathe out, I regulate the two centers. Then I inhale as I lift my hands and breathe out going down by the sides. Finally, I breathe in when I tie together and come back up with the hands; and breathe out as I push into the eyes. I make this exhalation last as long as possible; in this case, too, it should ideally accompany the movements until we come to the unbending intent.

THE CONTROL ON THE SECOND ATTENTION

I inhale as I grasp the area of unbending intent and then start an exhalation that ends when I am squatting down. I breathe freely while I keep the position. Then I breathe in as the arms open and exhale when they close in the area in front of the will.

COINCIDING WITH INTENT

As I get up leaning on the obtained density, I breathe in deeply; when the inhalation is ended, I hold my breath as I lift the hands and then exhale when the hands come back down the lateral flows.

I have to empty myself completely. This emptiness allows intent to access.

THE PERCEPTION OF THE DREAMER

Breathing freely, I stay in position for the time needed to access intent.

Then I inhale in two stages: the first part, as I lift my hand and turn my head; the second part is done as the hand passes before the eyes, the fingers hook onto and extract the eyes' fibers connected to the time line, and then the hand stops an instant on the other intensification point on the right. At that point ends the second part of the inhalation and I hold my breath for a moment.

Then I start breathing out while the head stays still and the hand continues along the time line, continuing to extract and extend the fibers from the eyes to their complete extension. This is the most important exhalation along the time line.

It is this exhalation that leads me to the dreamer's gaze. It needs to be precise, attentive to the details, especially the moment I open my hand.

I repeat it all starting on the left side.

RELEASING THE DREAMER'S MEMORIES

Lifting my hand, I breathe in. A long, controlled exhalation follows until I arrive at the knee. The exhalation should continue while I start stimulating the knee; then I breathe freely.

I repeat on the other side.

THE COINCIDENCE OF ATTENTION

I breathe in as I hook onto the sartorius muscle's fibers and lift the hands; I breathe out as I look for the exact position of the coincidence of attention at the confines of the luminous egg.

This exhalation gives us the right condition to find the correct point.

When I find it, I breathe in and out freely as I create the notch on the luminosity.

THE TEMPORARY DOUBLE

Lifting the hand, I breathe in and extract the fibers from the right eye. I breathe out as I place them, put them into the new position.

This breathing pattern is repeated in all of the positions on the right side as well as on the left: I breathe in as I extract the fibers and breathe out as I graft them into the new position.

The exhalation allows me to find the right placement.

COINCIDING WITH THE DOUBLE

I hold onto the corresponding point on the sartorius muscle that I have moved, and as I shift to the left I breathe in deeply; then, I breathe all the air out when I close the position with the left hand.

THE TWIN POSITION

I breathe freely as I settle into the twin position.

THE PREDOMINANCE OF THE ENERGY BODY

I turn to the right, breathe freely, inhale making one step forward, and exhale in the predominance of the energy body.

REFINEMENTS

This part of the book is a supplement to the first edition, aiming at clarifying some details in every single movement. So, I have added a suggestion, a further indication for each movement; what I deem useful for the next step.

My advice is, before you get to work and add them, learn the sequence well the way it is described in the previous part. Once you have acquired a deep knowledge of the movements and sensations you can relax and make space for you to focus on other details.

There are different reasons why these refinements were not present in the first edition; but the main one is that I have learned the sequence from inner silence, in terms of assemblage point positions; therefore, without a description.

At the time it was taught to me, I had to draw the physical movements from the continuity flows as exact sensations. Therefore, the need to describe the sequence through the common language had never arisen. I did it, and that was it.

Later on, when I have started conveying it to other people, I have needed a great "translation" work to obtain a description that was correct and understandable but would avoid dispersing, diminishing, or modifying the movements' energetic meaning. Therefore I acted cautiously and only used the descriptions whose effectiveness I was sure of, adding them a little at a time.

This is another piece of the description.

THE EARTH

The way we can hold and then fix the earth lines determines the precise attitude of the time mode in which we will perform the sequence.

What I refer to is the way you insert your hands into the density at the base of your feet, if you do it more or less quickly, how you move your fingers to latch onto and unite the earth lines to your intensity; then, how you select what you are moving, how you are holding it, how you lift it, the timing, the pauses, the breathing, the final closing, and the descent on to the will. In time you will realize that every detail in this initial phase decides all the rest, the whole execution of the sequence and, when this understanding becomes active, you can choose, devoid of thinking, the direction you give to the sequence every time.

And thus, also the intent it sustains.

It is not something that has to be looked for or built, or imagined; we only have to enjoy as much as possible every slightest detail of the initial movement.

THE DIRECTION

When you move your arms, starting from the will, to gather the vibratory center, actively look for the sensation of the fingers elongating all the way to the earth to gather and pull up.

They elongate, gather, rake, and then everything comes together in the vibratory aspect. It is something flexible.

THE CHANGE OF INTENSITY

Remember that preparatory inhalation, as we gather with our hands and lift them to form a window, must be very deep, so that the exhalation may be prolonged and modulated in order to guarantee the expulsion of the inner dialogue.

The exhalation is extremely controlled: it really must expel the inner dialogue.

While we breathe out, our back adjusts itself: the area of unbending intent, the wings of perception.

We find the position by doing the micro-movements that fix the back, settling all unbalances. As we “push” forward the expulsion of the inner dialogue, we use this force to obtain inner continuity flows that work on the physical configuration of the back and then of the hips and legs.

It is not imaginary, we really have to feel the bones falling into place, assuming a correct posture, so as to correspond to the force of silence.

Use the arms as a perfectly balanced counterweight that regulates itself and regulates your configuration.

The spine adjusts itself, also affecting the area of the glow (that corresponds to the vertebrae at the base of the nape), the area of unbending intent, and connecting this adjustment through the legs all the way to the grounding to the earth.

Maintain absolute silence during this operation.

THE ATTENTION BEYOND THE LIMITS

Continue adjusting the back. The internal continuity flows that are released spread out throughout the body. It is a fundamental moment to ensure that we never get blocked, that we use this mobility of the internal continuity flows to make them reverberate in the body, keeping it active.

We should never crystallize any position.

Maintain inner mobility, which reflects on the external one.

The opening of the arms works deeply on the wings of perception. The shoulder blades must work by closing as the chest opens.

THE SENSITIVITY OF THE VIBRATORY CENTER

When we extend, we reach the limits of the luminous egg, where we have created the dome of luminosity with the earth lines. Let us try feeling that there is a precise point in which the hands cross an invisible, but clear-cut limit. What we find in that thickness is very precious and is what we bring into the vibratory aspect.

These movements also have the purpose of processing these fractions of intensity and acquire them into our energy configuration, matching and harmonizing them to our energy fibers.

THE DISCIPLINE OF ACTIONS – PATIENCE - THE PREPARATION

During these phases you can learn the correct eye-mobility, the one associated to the internal continuity flows.

Hook the eyes onto the movement; but not in the sense that you move the eyes. The mobility I am talking about is not "moving the ocular bulbs." It is softness.

The correct way of explaining it is saying that, while I do the physical movements, I "see" my continuity flows. I apply the double perception: I gaze with continuity at what I look at and, at the same time, I have the full perception of the effect of the sequence on the configuration of the internal emanations.

This perceptual condition gives me the sensation of moving the eyes in strange "soft" trajectories.

As I come down and go back up again I open and adjust my back.

When the hands come down by the sides, they have to be "inserted" into an already existing space, an emptiness that separates the layers of the luminous egg.

CALLING THE WORLD FORTH - RECEIVING THE WORLD

Use these movements to refine, confirm your ability to find and use the "open passages" in the area of possibilities.

The sequence wholly unfurls in these open passages that we call "continuity gaps," which we meet when we explore the area of possibilities.

They are called continuity gaps because they are perceived as actual free passages in the density of the area of possibilities; and because, when one is picked, it is possible to continue following it without interruption. In their most extreme application, they can lead our entire totality through passages to the second attention.

The sequence is something "already present," meaning that it is the codification of a series of continuity gaps guided by a very precise intent. Using the continuity gaps with the right type of attention causes the movement of the assemblage point. The use of continuity gaps can take place physically but also by simply intending it, or in other forms that become ever more mysterious, approaching the modes of the blue worlds.

In practice, all of this translates into the fact that our body moves alone, with lightness, as though an air current transported it. The arms are lifted, the hands fine-tune extremely precise details that have consequences on our state and do it within this sensation of exactly defined open space. If we get out of this space, so precisely defined, the intensity ends, it is lost.

Thanks to their natural fluidity, these two movements are particularly suited to the purpose of finding the continuity gaps;

but the same elegance and smoothness must accompany every part of the sequence.

This way of moving involves the whole body at the same moment, in the same movement, not only the arms.

The continuity gaps are unified, extended to the whole body by the internal continuity flows.

THE DISCIPLINE OF UNBENDING INTENT

As I move by the area of unbending intent, I linger there a moment to look for, find, and firmly grab the foundation of unbending intent and drag it toward the earth.

Also remember that every time you slide down the legs with your hands you are intervening to release accumulated memories; especially in this passage over the back of your legs, in which you apply the discipline of unbending intent to the conduction of the memories themselves.

The same thing happens as you come back up, adding the earth's guide, too.

As you do the recapitulation you will find the improvement induced by this movement's intent.

As you go down and up, try to keep such a stance as to involve and use the legs, allowing strength and relaxed tension flow in them, firmly maintaining your grounding with the earth. You will succeed better in this if you will continue keeping your back straight and gaze forward.

INNER STRENGTH

When the hands rest on the vibratory flow, they must really lean on it. The arms are relaxed, with elbows lowered, relaxed, as though we were resting with our hands on something solid.

Continue adjusting your back and whole body to the balance produced by the arms.

The hands designing a butterfly connect the earth lines to the vibratory center, use them to ignite the vibratory aspect and then spread them throughout the vibratory aspect. In other words: what is gathered, condensed, and channeled by the hands as they design a butterfly must then flow in the area of possibilities, in the whole, extended body.

It starts as a nucleus of intensity that has been gathered; but what you must intend is that the inner strength contained in this nucleus should start flowing, like blood in the double perception's veins, and spread uniformly in the area of possibilities.

Apply this inner force at once, use patience, allow it time to occur.

CONTROL

We have to push with our hands slightly turned downward. If we really feel the presence of the nucleus of intensity, we can govern it, hold it firmly without losing it.

We must not hurry, there is always a right time, different every time, that allows us to transfer it into the will. Also when we get on the will, we have to make sure we let it settle before moving on to the next movement.

THE INFALLIBLE GUIDE

The movements of the hands must be emphasized and performed with the maximum focus so that they can be transmitted through the arms, all the way to the back. You have to feel the tendons working and bridging the other parts of the body.

At the end, we receive the boost in the back, as well as in the will; and there is a balance between all the centers. The use of the final act is also to obtain balance between the different aspects of the energy outlined by the power centers.

THE REALIGNMENT

When I make my hands come up the sides, the fingers gather the qualities of attention relevant to dreaming and seeing, unifying and extending them forward and transferring them into the flow of the vibratory center. Also in this case, as I move the hands along the sides, I induce a special shiver that I accompany with my hands, that flows together with my hands.

I continue using the balance of the arms to harmonize the alignment of the back and the whole body. A high physical sensitivity is needed to seize and use every minimal impulse to obtain this reconfiguration.

The hands in the shape of a butterfly connect the earth lines to the vibratory center and then spread them throughout the whole vibratory aspect.

The same happens when we bring the nucleus of density obtained from the emanations outside back to the vibratory center. Here come also into play aspects of intent (that come from outside with the return wave), unintelligible to the linear mind, that merge with the vibratory aspect.

The entire nucleus of intensity must be pushed down with care until we make it merge with the will.

EXTENDING UNBENDING INTENT

The movements we make with our hands to unify the aspects of intent and the vibratory aspect with the will are not codified. They change every time we do the sequence, depending on the way we have led it up to that moment.

It is another movement in which we can fine-tune, confirm the continuity gaps. The hands slide easily along the open lines, glide in the flows without interruption. It is important that, when we move the hands up and then slide them in front of the will and the center for decisions, they move coming up along the sides with precision. We have to find the open space between the layers of the luminous egg. These spaces correspond to the continuity gaps.

THE OPENING

In this phase, the perception is modified in a special form. Just when we are pushing the two sides apart, there is a moment in which the world has something like a glitch. It disappears for an almost imperceptible instant, and then it reappears. The opening, the separation of the left and right sides carries with it the awareness that the alignment is continuously renewed: it actually appears and disappears without a break. This is what gives us the sensation that there is a "time passing;" but it is a trick, an illusion. What we perceive as linear time is, in reality, the world as alignment that repeats itself.

Afterwards, during the rest of the sequence this perception can return at different moments.

The hands must then turn outward, in correspondence of the two intensification points, so that the back can fully work. The shoulder blades close as we turn the hands and then open when we spread out the arms.

THE LINES OF FORCE

Every time I pass over the head with my hands "I lower the visor."

The sensation corresponds to hooking onto something behind the nape, in the area of the glow, and dragging it more or less to the level of the time line. It is like a transparent membrane that is unfolded until it covers the head and produces silence.

It is the special quality of silence that is obtained from the area of the glow.

The connection with the suggester is severed with this act.

The connection created by inserting the essence of the wings of perception into the lateral flows causes a series of very precious adjustments in our perceptual possibility.

Such adjustments are clearly perceived as we go down the lateral flows. These are changes, shifts, which may be minimal but distinguishable in the way our perception is functioning, even just our visual or auditory perception (but the effect can be transferred to the expanded perception).

Train yourself to detect them, even by repeating the step over and over. This will further fine-tune your ability to intensify attention.

THE CHANGE IN DIRECTION

Before starting coming back up with the hands, I also latch onto the two lower intensification points in order to bring the effect back to the center for decisions.

Clearly, when I separate the two sides, the same condition described in *The Opening* takes place. Actually the repeating alignment, the appearance and disappearance of the world, should become even easier to recognize. Indeed, the function of the reiteration of the same movement is precisely to corroborate its effect and, since obtaining the awareness of the full and the empty alternating in the world's continuity is essential for warriors, the separation of the two sides is confirmed a second time.

Such awareness is of capital importance also because it concerns the distinction between tonal and nagual. Tonal and nagual alternate in this appearing and disappearing.

It is the dynamics that renews the world.

OPENING THE LEFT SIDE

The role of the legs is essential. As always, they are not inert but, in particular during this phase, they have the task of compensating, balancing the modifications in the internal configuration brought by the opening of the left side. They form a system of balance together with the right hand, a system that gets reorganized, adapting and compensating the impulses to the continuity flows obtained as we weld the left side with the emanations outside.

Thus, the legs are not at all inactive: they gather the variations and transmit them into the earth. From it they obtain responses that go through the body and reach the left side, actively participating in the process that is being carried out.

All of this happens physically; there must be a real, physical effort. If there is none, it is because we are doing something wrong.

The sequence makes it very clear that warriors need a resilient, trained, physically reactive but flexible body.

The nature of the confrontation with infinity is not intellectual.

THE GAZE BEYOND INTERPRETATION

In all of the movements of the sequence, the arms are always soft, although provided with relaxed tension, just like the whole body. When we extend the arm toward the direction of the rolling force, we do not extend it completely, that is, all the joints are slightly and naturally bent, which allows the attention to flow.

When the arm has reached its final extension we feel a continuity, a flowing from the immense distance, which we are looking at, to inside the earth, through the continuity with the right hand. This flow is modulated, governed, by the area of the glow and by the wings of perception.

It is this continuity that "releases" the rolling force, that makes it start.

EXPANDING THE LEFT SIDE

We exploit the opening of the left side to extend the main centers. Being already welded to the emanations outside, the maneuver works out easily. Exploit the sensation that is already available to you. It is like inserting into the sensation of opening and uniting the left side other, more precise details, filaments, lines, flows that join this mix.

The impression of a physical modification of the body becomes more evident. The hand goes down (again, along the natural weld) every time we change point, settling at the level of the next one. If you pay attention, you will realize that the hand tends to stop of its own accord at the correct height to reach the next center. So, the location of the centers will be even clearer.

When we get to the will, we also include the lower intensification point.

For women, it is possible to include the womb with an additional movement.

THE PROTECTED STANCE

Before pushing on the time line and then turning toward the rolling force, we do a small but important regulation of the relationship between the eyes and the time line.

Let the hand act alone, guided by the will and by the way your body feels that the regulation is right. When it is correct, the body relaxes.

Therefore, you must have first acquired a kind of special tension that is a sort of "will to carry out a precise gesture." This tension is charged during the extension of the left side and lifts the hand, positioning it correctly on the time line.

THE ROLLING FORCE

Remember that now you are slightly shifted to the side with respect to the opening that allows to harmonize the rolling force.

Thus, the attention is shifted to the right eye.

The right and left sides become defined and differentiated.

The right and left eyes become defined and differentiated.

This difference is then confirmed in *The Maneuverability of the Vibratory Aspect* and persists throughout the rest of the sequence. It is essential to use it immediately after the rolling force (precisely, in *The Maneuverability of the Vibratory Aspect*), in order to define it; and then, toward the end of the sequence, when we produce the temporary double by shifting the centers.

The left side is like empty, separate, isolated with respect to the right side, as though there were a solid, insuperable limit that divides the two sides and continues to infinity, maintaining the boost of the rolling force in the right side.

Still, the left side remains open, but on an isolated space that allows to quickly escape, to move in zero time.

When we rotate in the harmonization phase, we control the effect of the rolling force and use it to reconfigure the right side in a totally new way.

It is what leads to harmonizing nagual and tonal.

NOT INDULGING

A double control level is implemented. This means that, on one side, we shift the direction of the attention, seal a passage, creating a protection that allows us to focus on a completely different direction than the one we were facing one moment before. On the other side, however, we also continue maintaining control over what is beyond the door that we have closed on the left side.

The sensation is that a piece, a level, a quality, or a trait of our totality has remained "there." It is like having awareness of two sides at the same time. One, the one that is now in front of us after we have turned, is very solid, concrete, clearly defined: it is tonal.

The other one, the one that is "beyond," that has remained beyond that limit we have closed, has indefinable traits; it is adaptable, elusive, in spite of being endowed with absolute clarity.

In this way, we define the domains of tonal and nagual after having harmonized them.

The fact of leaving something in a precise level also prepares the sensation that we will use in *The Space for the New Positions*.

Physically, it is perceived just like a "second body" that remains in that position, that parts from us as we turn to the right.

THE MANEUVERABILITY OF THE VIBRATORY ASPECT

As I follow with my eyes the lines connecting the areas of peripheral perception, the eyes become definitively differentiated. The right and left eyes glide in different ways, or better: producing different sensitivities. The idea is that they slide on parallel tracks that, however, have slightly different speed, varying from each other but never coinciding.

Again we start from the concept of having a soft mobility of the eyes as a sensation.

This mobility is governed by the will, which is connected to the eyes.

As they move in this way, the eyes confirm the directions, without us thinking it, seizing highly defined but minimal points along their paths.

If it is fluid and natural, the eye movement frees the area of the glow. We feel that the area below the nape of the neck completely relaxes, allowing intensity currents to pass.

OPENING THE TIME LINE

Also in this movement I "lower the visor" and continue settling the back.

The hands position themselves exactly underneath the eyes. The thumbs are open at the sides of the head, the other fingers are united, well-extended. There must be a tension flowing to form a continuous ring from the shoulder blades to the tip of the fingers, which stay separate. Hands and elbows are more or less at the same height.

The gaze slides on the back of the hands and moves further: it intends the creation of and endless horizon. The will supports the palms of the hands, creating a surface on which they can lean and then start gliding, opening and expanding the horizon.

I should feel myself being lifted, becoming lighter as I extend the arms.

THE TIME NICHE

When I go down into the dreaming niche, I drag the extension of the time line with me.
I do it in an elegant, docile way, caressing it and attracting it down.
In other words, the position is not down there; it is I who take it down there from the horizon of extended time.

When I am down in position, my way of looking searches for the emanations outside, beyond the description. The gaze contains the intent of going beyond what I materially see, to go behind, where there is no description. This trains me to spontaneously apply seeing to dreaming.

TIMING OR THE STALKER'S HARMONY

When the hand darts down to capture the quotas of attention, we have to use the "controlled rapid movements." I will try to explain what it is, although it is not simple. Here I can only give you the main indications.
These movements also occur in the area of possibilities, springing from the natural coordination between the will and unbending intent. They require a "charge" that is produced by the internal continuity flows and is then released in a precise movement, endowed with purpose, direction, relaxed force, and that develops in the continuity gaps.
The purpose of the gesture is given by the interaction between the will and unbending intent.

The direction results from the exact coincidence with the area of possibilities.

The relaxed force is given by the application of the first two attributes of stalking.

Here we could also say that the controlled rapid movements are the physical expression (but actually not only physical) of the first two attributes of stalking, preceded by the other two: forbearance and timing, which actually generate them.

In practice, and in the specific case, the arm that must go to seize the quotas of attention receives and uses the impulse that comes from the central part of the body, which is very intense. This would lead us to making an excessive gesture; that is why control and discipline are applied at once to it (as we are abandoned in the act).

Thus, the hand slows down in the exact point where it must and in the way it has to do it.

In fact, it actually slows down already from the moment the movement begins, progressively, almost imperceptibly.

The controlled rapid movements are used in very many steps in the sequence, not only in this case. From here on, I will point them out to you. Keep in mind that they are also used in *The Rolling Force – The Preparation* and in *The Protected Stance*, when going down, when changing sides, and when getting up. In *The Protected Stance* they apply to the whole body.

The controlled rapid movements are part of the "Right Way of Moving."

THE PRINCIPLES OF STALKING

I apply the controlled rapid movements, both when I grab and when I fling upwards as I get up. In this case, the controlled rapid movements are applied to the whole body.

What we fling upwards accompanies then the hands to grasp the wings of perception correctly.

THE QUOTAS OF ATTENTION

I lower the visor.

I grab the quotas of attention with the controlled rapid movements.

When I position myself on the time line, the hands are placed as previously described in *Opening the Time Line*; thus, immediately below the eyes, with thumbs open at the sides of the face and hands with united and extended fingers. I form a ring of force with the elbows and shoulder blades that helps me focus on the fringes of the peripheral perception.

The hands and arms glide inside a passage, at whose end are the quotas of attention. They do not extend completely straight, I keep a minimum, natural arch in the joints.

Also when I bring the quotas of attention to the center for decisions the hands glide, as though they were attracted by the center itself.

While I let the quotas be absorbed, the elbows are relaxed, but never deprived of force.

The second time, the movement gets activated thanks to a particular connection between the will, unbending intent, and upper intensification points. At a precise moment, when the intensity is correct, these latch onto and drag the hands to flow toward the quotas of attention.

THE FINE-TUNING

The fine-tuning is the discipline of sentiments.

THE SPACE FOR THE NEW POSITIONS

When the eight movements for the stalker's space are made, the gaze must be kept at infinity. Avoid focusing your attention on the hands. Look at the space between, launching the attention forward, to infinity. You already have to look in this way as you have your hands on the area of unbending intent and not allow the arrival of the blow of your hands to distract you in the least.

At the same time, you bring the peripheral perception to the whole area external to the hands.

Thus, you obtain a diversified perceptual order that allows you to use the double perception.

The purpose is to catch, in the peripheral perception, the effect of the hands' blow on the confines of the luminous egg. A vibration or a translucent halo is produced in the area in front of us, expanding from there. There is correspondence in the will.

As I turn, I must maintain a continuous gaze and then anchor it with absolute immediacy to the area that will be central at the moment I will hit with my hands. I anchor the gaze to this area and immediately I launch the attention to infinity.

These are all controlled rapid movements, including the shifts on the legs.

THE NEW ALIGNMENT

This is the ideal moment to go in depth into the subject of "internal continuity flows."

Accessing the internal continuity flows means, very briefly put, to shift into the condition that allows us to perceive the changes in the relationship between the emanations inside, between the energy fibers that make us up. The perception of such changes takes place as flows or movement and can take on many forms, from a physical "feeling" to "seeing" the currents, the variations in configuration, like some sort of circulation and organization of forces, or energy.

It is possible to access this type of condition only by using the double perception applied to ourselves as a group of emanations.

Moving in the area of possibilities is probably the best way to train to obtain this state, and it allows to translate the perception of the internal continuity flows into body movements.

In the movement that we are examining there are two moments particularly suited for sensing the internal continuity flows. The first is when we stand still with hands and arms creating a space to be filled; and the second is when the twist is reaching its maximum point and we stop. In both cases, we can shift the attention to the way the internal continuity flows (meaning, internal to the luminous egg) reorganize the energy configuration.

Obviously, the entire sequence should be done with the awareness of the internal continuity flows.

The disciplined translation of the internal continuity flows into body movements is part of the right way of moving.

IGNITING WITH THE EARTH

As we bend down we use controlled rapid movements. We must "hold" our back, not let ourselves fall like a dead weight. In other words, we have to let go with total abandonment, but by applying control.

The legs are stretched, you have to feel the back tendons working.

When we come back up, the vertebral spine straightens up "unrolling;" that is, we start lifting ourselves up from the first, lower vertebrae and then coming up all the way to the nape of the neck, whose vertebrae will be the last ones to realign. It is like a wave lifting us with a precise order.

Thus, the head stays lowered up to the last moment.

This way of coming back up (also) helps to unblock the area of the glow.

Remember, when you lift your hands, to drag also at the two upper points of intensification of the attention.

The legs are straight, we have to feel the back of the legs pulling. It is this tension that allows to latch onto the earth lines and to let them flow.

THE CHANGE

When I position myself again, the hands and arms go slowly down the sides.

The hands glide down the farthest limits of the peripheral vision.

This descent is a form of coordination, an exact fine-tuning of the precise attitudes of the time modes. Every time we do the sequence, at this point we fine-tune our ability to obtain coherence within a time mode, an alignment. It is perceived as an adjustment in the whole body of the internal continuity flows; and we realize that the way we control the descent of the arms regulates, guides this adjustment.

THE EFFECT OF SILENCE

When we grasp the nucleus of the inner dialogue and drag it to the other side, we must not lose sight of it. We keep our eyes directed at, focused on the nucleus that we hold in our hand. And we follow its disruption when we blow it away to disperse it.

THE SLIDING DOORS

We go back to considering the lower part of the body, remembering, first of all, that it is never idle. The legs work for the whole duration of the sequence in a similar position as the one called “the horseman” in martial arts: similar, but not exactly the same.

In the sequence we stand a bit taller; however, the idea is always to keep a perfect grounding, the back straight, aligned.

In the sequence the positioning of the body parts must be such as to allow us to find a dynamic stability that engages us thoroughly, yet without causing tensions or disharmony. Keep in mind that this position is not static; it continuously modifies itself with respect to and offsetting the variations of the energy configuration. The change in posture is often externally unnoticeable, but continuous.

The leg and hip joints are, in any case, always bent. During this phase, conversely, legs and hips straighten up.

Careful: they are not stiff, tense, they stay relaxed; yet, they continue working, responding to the internal continuity flows.

GOVERNING SILENCE

The legs are still straight, but relaxed and active.

The hands slide naturally into the two frontal, lateral flows. Therefore, in the previous movements, in which the two frontal flows are involved, I must have made their position and type of intensity very clear. The hands settle in the right place, attracted and held by the details of the intensity of the lateral flows.

The intent is to refine the silence, purify it, make it crystal-clear and abstract.

OPENING SILENCE

The legs are still straight, but relaxed and active.

My personal silence, which I gathered earlier, is released and merges with the silence of the world. They become a single thing, without confines.

The opening of the left side, which I had previously made, and which I am now facing, helps me obtain the coincidence and the amalgamation of the world's silence with mine.

This is of the utmost importance. It is the act that will allow me to obtain inner silence directly from the world, instead of fighting to impose it to myself.

I learn to be yielding, to allow the world to help me. I learn it in the body, not by trying to understand "how it is done."

THE EXTENSION OF SILENCE

The legs and pelvis return to the bent and grounded position they had kept throughout the rest of the sequence.

The position I take helps me activate the silence I have just gathered and connected with the world's silence. Be aware that, in *The Availability of Intent*, I will use this elaborate silence to relate with the active side of infinity, identify it, be able to interact with it.

Therefore, I explore with perceptual continuity the part of the time line limited by the hands, charging it with active silence, or charging silence with the reactivity of the time line.

Then I release it all and guide it toward infinity.

We gaze at the horizon of silence, until it pushes on the hands.

THE NOT-DOING OF THE SELF

While I wait for the nucleus of the self that I have to dissolve with the sweeping breath, I look for a precise sensation. I need the hand that I hold up to capture a social node.

The sensation is that there is a current flowing between the fingers and that, at a given moment, there is a denser core that "gets wedged" in the space between the central fingers, as though the hand were a rake. This is the core I hold and then elaborate with the sweeping breath.

The way we use our eyes is crucial.

The gaze is always continuous when we move our head in the sweeping breath. What I mean is that the eyes look ahead, not moving jerkily, but sliding on everything we have in front, registering every detail. We cross our eyes for an instant the moment when, in the sweeping breath, we face the hand (when it is at the center of the face), making it slide softly from the expanded vision to the focused, and then again to the expanded.

THE AVAILABILITY OF INTENT

When looking between the fingers, the space between works as a lens. We look for the precise angle that puts intent in focus.

The moment we sense it, the perception defines an area, a small zone at hand, highly defined and separate from the rest of space.

It is like a small piece endowed with greater reality, as though it had depth and dimension, and the rest were flat. It is an aspect of the living world, reactive, endowed with "intelligence."

It is what we grasp and pull with our hands.

We use only one eye at a time, alternating the right and left eye, to separate and define the characteristics of the two sides. The eye we do not use stays covered by the hand.

THE TIME OF INFINITY

The hands must go down to the vibratory center and the will, resting on a common plane, in a perfect axis. Pretend you have your hands resting on a board that pivots around the center for decisions and goes down toward the will.

Thus, they move slightly forward, outwards, and then come down.

The fingers are open, extended. The thumb of the right hand and the little finger of the left hand are aligned.

As I regulate the two centers, there must be a clear variation in the perception, a refinement. There is a correspondence between what I do with my hands, the way the eyes move, and the perceptual variation. I realize I can affect in detail my perceptual condition through the slightest movement of my hands.

When I move on to regulating the other centers, the hands are dragged by the anticipatory effect, by the real time effect. What truly happens is that the movement of the hands "has already happened" a moment before. From this ensues a kind of inevitability of the movement, the fact that the hands are doing what they actually have already done.

THE CONTROL ON THE SECOND ATTENTION

We have to wait for the space contained by the arms and legs to become so loaded as to induce the hands to open, lift up, and thus position themselves at the correct height to lean and slide on the plane of intensity and effectiveness that is created.

The gliding of the hands and arms confirms the level we can use as a stable supporting surface to lift ourselves.

COINCIDING WITH INTENT

At the moment in which they have to rest, the hands come close to the face and take the same position, just underneath the eyes and the time line, already adopted in other passages of the sequence: thumbs extended at the sides of the face, fingers united and extended just under the eyes. However, they are a little more detached from the face, in two frontal flows.

For a moment I should feel the strength that comes from the coincidence between the lateral flows and the time line. It is what I use to lift myself, keeping the right alignment.

As I lift myself, the hands stay still where they are, absolutely still; they do not follow the lifting of the rest of the body at all.

Only once I have gotten up, settled and stopped, then my hands come up along the lateral flows and go back down again to the two lower intensification points.

THE PERCEPTION OF THE DREAMER

The gaze is continuous as I move my head; it slides, looking beyond.

The eyes are slightly crossed when the hand moves in front of them and they govern, or are governed, by what the hand moves.

This fine-tuning allows to see the repetition of the dreamer in the layers of awareness.

The sensation, the moment our gaze goes beyond the hand, is like going out in an open space from a closed one; that the hand removes a veil, an obstacle that prevented us from having a lucid and deep sight.

It is the feeling of looking straight into the time line, inside the time line; all the way to the infinite horizon, beyond, beyond... but straight at eye level, without dispersing the attention, focusing on the distance.

RELEASING THE DREAMER'S MEMORIES

This is one of the moments in which, most of all, it is essential to follow the spaces of minor resistance in the area of possibilities. The continuity gaps must be followed in every movement, every detail of the sequence. This, however, is the moment it becomes evident whether we are doing it or not, since it is absolutely essential to find and follow the lines that lead us correctly to the knee.

If we do not reach it in this fashion, it will not be possible to stimulate it and release the dreamer's memories.

We have to wait and let the arm rise only when it is lifted by an ascending flow (similar to the updraft when opening the left side), we follow it and it gets naturally inserted into the lateral flow that connects all of the centers. So, the arm is moved by a force that seems to be independent of us.

The arm bends on the time line, goes down a diagonal that attracts it to the knee, which is stimulated correctly only if we are yielding, willing to trust the will; without thinking about how we should do it, but applying an active attention that transfers the dreamer's memories.

Do not look at the knee as you stimulate it. Instead, apply your double perception.

THE COINCIDENCE OF ATTENTION

The moment we begin pushing inside the layers of the luminous egg, the point of the second attention on the right side must activate the center for decisions.

The hands find the right point by following the details of the type of intensity, like it happens when we insert them into the lateral flows in *Governing Silence*.

THE TEMPORARY DOUBLE

The attention must be completely shifted on the side on which we are working. It is like feeling continuously unbalanced, first on the right side and then, after turning around, on the left; it is as though the opposite side to the one in which I create the temporary double did not exist physically anymore.

There is a precise line of attention, which is the one where we form the temporary double; and it corresponds to the intuited limit of the peripheral perception. The more our hand goes back, to the limit of the possibility of our peripheral vision and more into feeling, the better it works.

Women can also insert the womb into the creation of the temporary double.

Every time I place a part, the hand goes down to the next level along the axis of the limit of perception. If we are abandoned and attentive, the hand will go down and then stop naturally at the exact point, without us trying to think where it is.

COINCIDING WITH THE DOUBLE

After moving to the side and closing the opening, look for the sensation of finding yourself in a different world. In "another" place; other in terms of alignment.

The opening we close is the same we had opened on the left side, through which we had evoked the rolling force and from which we obtained the coincidence of the silence of the world. Now we are the ones "on the other side," we do not look "from outside" anymore, but are inside and close the passage to the world we know.

Now, it is the known alignment that becomes "the other side."

As we unite with the temporary double, we let the awareness slide in the earth, like at the beginning.

The area of the glow gets totally freed.

THE PREDOMINANCE OF THE ENERGY BODY

In order to obtain the clear perception of the presence of the energy body, I have to use non-gazing. If we look at the concrete objects beyond the point in which it should be, our attention is not working correctly.

I have to focus my attention, hold it in the space between me and the point in which the energy body should be.

Using the attention in this way causes the will to transform the space in question. A special quality of awareness, tied to the nagual, is concentrated there.

After some time, longer or shorter, the presence of an entity is formed at the opposite limit of this area of awareness.

It is a human entity, but at the same time it is not, it is savage, but endowed with a higher and unfathomable discipline. It is us, but we are alien to ourselves.

It is more real than what I believe I am. It is real to the utmost, uncorrupted, crystal clear, with a sincerity, an authenticity that terrorizes and moves me at the same time.

It is not necessary to "see" it, but to perceive it.

At the end we move at the same time as the other and we "wear" it, like clothing.

SPECIAL EXECUTIONS

IN THE DARK

Once the movements are firmly acquired in the body and it is thus possible to execute them by wholly excluding the mental interference, it is possible to do some special executions of the sequence.

One of these is done in the darkness. In this execution, we can keep our eyes indifferently open or closed; in either case, the type of perception we use as we move is completely different from the ordinary one. Doing the sequence in the dark is very useful. First of all, it puts us in the ideal condition for developing the precise awareness of the way our body moves and positions itself. We cannot rely on our sight, we have to be in the body.

It also allows us to acquire the necessary state of perception, which we apply then to every kind of execution: the perception of the internal continuity flows within the area of possibilities.

When the silence really comes, we start "seeing" the formation of luminous lines and areas that accompany our movements and connect them without a break. In the end, the execution in the dark leads up to the exact perception of the continuity gaps.

WITH THE SHADOW

Another one of the special executions is the one with one's shadow.

It is very simple but enormously effective under many aspects, especially with respect to the ability to clearly perceive the effects of the movements on the different power centers.

To do it, you need a source of grazing light (like that of the sun at sunset) and a surface on which our shadow can be cast. This surface must be in front of us at such a distance as to produce a life-size shadow or little bigger. It can be vertical or slightly slanted. A smooth rock face or a grassy embankment would be ideal.

We place ourselves in front of this surface with the source of light on our back and keep, as a gazing point, the area corresponding to the vibratory center in the projection of our shadow. Then, we simply do the sequence.

What we look for in this type of execution is a greater and more precise perception of the connections and the sensitivity between the different layers of the luminous egg, including the physical body. The shadow works as a mirror of our perceptions; by gazing at it, we can "see" exactly what really happens and transfer this heightened perception in terms of sensations to our body. It also becomes a great deal easier to view the shifts of the energy fibers induced by the movements of the sequence.

When we turn and, thus, our shadow is behind our back, we must continue keeping a sensitive connection with the shadow through the sensation that the shadow reflects into our areas of intense perception, especially into the area of the shoulder blades, the wings of perception that are connected to the vibratory center. This also helps unfolding the wings of perception.

When the shadow is at our side, we use the expanded perception and the peripheral vision.

DEFINING A FUNDAMENTAL ASPECT

Releasing the area of the glow.

There are a few benchmarks in the sequence, some essential conditions that we have to learn to develop and sustain throughout the duration of the execution, without need to think about them, to continuously focus on them. They must flow together with the sequence, uplift it. They help taking it to progressive levels.

Indeed, they are the cherry on the cake, what makes the difference between “executing the sequence” and “being the sequence.”

They are maintained throughout the whole sequence.

An example I can bring is freeing the area of the glow, but only as an example, so that it may be clearer for you how we can develop these crucial points.

Well, actually, there is another reason why I specifically chose freeing the area of the glow as an example of a fundamental aspect. It is the evolutionary action that more than any other brings about the predominance of the energy body.

When we decide to use the sequence to define a fundamental aspect, the principle is to execute it only with that purpose, from the beginning to the end; thus, recalling and maintaining that specific intent.

The simplest way to recall and maintain the specific intent is to do it by using the body, instead of setting oneself to search for who-knows-what "magic." It is a great deal more immediate and real, effective. Moreover, it moves us onto the body that, being our true mind, knows well what we look for and what to do.

In the case of the area of the glow, what we focus on is a very precise, physical sensation: the loosening and flowing of the area at the nape of the neck, the sensation that it becomes liquid, soft; that we can feel disciplined, mild, yielding currents flowing through it. The moment in which we seize the exact sensation is marked by a precise sentiment, a special kind of emotional and even physical stir that reaches the eyes. It is similar to when we start crying, but it is not that. In fact, it moves then to the top of the head, where it takes on a different character, abstract and uninterested. Then, many things can happen, but this is a different story.

Let us go back to the execution.

In the specific case of freeing the area of the glow, already as we are standing, at the start, waiting to be pulled down by the earth lines, we dedicate our full attention to developing and maintaining this sensation and we never cease. We substitute all of the other sensations with this one, as the dominant sensation.

Defining the fundamental aspects requires to have already acquired the ability to do the sequence without thinking, with the body moving in the sensations without looking for them. In this way, we can shift and hold our attention on the new sensation: the one we want to define as the fundamental aspect.

The following are some of the main, fundamental aspects; others will appear in time, as you develop your intimacy with the sequence.

- **Moving in the area of possibilities**
- **Using the double perception / perceiving the internal continuity flows**
- **Following the continuity gaps**
- **Associating the mobility of the eyes with the movements / obtaining malleability in the gaze**
- **Using the legs / obtaining continuity with the earth**
- **Connecting eyes and will**
- **Maintaining the silence**
- **Freeing the unbending intent**
- **Releasing the wings of perception**
- **Freeing the vibratory aspect**

I will stop here, it seems that there is enough work, for now.

USING THE SINGLE MOVEMENTS OR PARTS OF THE SEQUENCE

Every single movement of the sequence has its specific effectiveness, a precise intent that one can resort to independently of the execution of the entire sequence. The single movements are used for their specific purpose; thus, not for the purpose of obtaining the predominance of the energy body; however, they are useful when we need help, an extra boost, to settle in a direction, find clarity again, etc. The purposes are infinite.

With the same goal, we can also use parts of the sequence, instead of the single movements.

Naturally, in order to learn to seize these multiple purposes, it is essential to have acquired a good mastery in executing the whole sequence.

On the other hand, it is also true that using the single movements helps us fine-tuning them and catch the infinite nuances, which results then in greater effectiveness when executing the complete sequence.

INTENDING THE SEQUENCE

Intending the sequence means executing it without doing the movements; thus, keeping still, simply intending it.

You can do it standing up, sitting, or lying down. I find that the best way is to do it comfortably seated in my recapitulation environment, inside a dark and small place, like the recapitulation tent, box, a small natural cavity, or other environments with the right characteristics. The recapitulation tent, to give you an idea, has these dimensions: 1 meter times 1 meter times 1.7-1.8 meters.

This environment, restricted and dark, gives cohesion to and reorganizes the emanations. The resulting effect is better access to the double perception and the area of possibilities.

We can also improve our ability to maintain our attention.

Irrespective of how we settle ourselves to execute the sequence by intending it, we have to be able to transfer onto the body, maintain silence, and feel the same sensations we feel when we do the sequence by moving.

Initially, we will do it in a way that is very similar to creating a sort of projection of ourselves doing the movements, a projection we create with our body. Essentially, it becomes like performing it through a double. Done this way, it is also a way to stimulate and guide the creation of a double, a dreaming body.

Naturally, this kind of execution requires that we have first reached an excellent mastery of the movements and sensations in the normal execution; we must have come to the point of not having to think them, to the point in which the body knows them and there is no more mental intervention.

This way of doing it is very important because it allows to reach an extreme clarity concerning the exact sensations to look for.

The best way to intend the sequence, however, is not by trying to visualize the movements. It would keep us pinned down to a type of mental, material concentration, tied to the description; whereas what we are looking for is the exact opposite: moving into the area of possibilities, shifting attention on the world as a sensation, and using the double perception to see the active energy flows.

Indeed, the correct mode consists in intending the sequence evoking the body sensations and thus producing the correspondent assemblage point shifts.

The following is the sequence in the form of guiding sensations. They correspond to the movements, but allow you to sublimate the strictly physical aspect and transfer yourself into the sensation and direct perception of the effects of the sequence.

I chose a specific type of sensations-perceptions and have done it for a precise reason: the guide I made shifts your attention on the balance of amber and blue energy. Obtaining the correct relationship between these two types of energy in the predominance of the energy body, makes us acquire indispensable characteristics to face the challenge of the unknown: characteristics of resilience, clarity, but also sweetness and cunning, timing, strategy, and the ability to intuit the "right" directions.

You can let a friend help you from outside the tent (or the place in which you are doing the intended sequence), who reads slowly, with the right pauses, the following text. Or make a recording that you fine-tune each time to obtain the right effect.

In this way, you are guided without having to think and remember.

The Guiding Sensations

- I relax, search for silence, slow down the restlessness of the emanations inside. I let them go downward, until they are latched on by heavier lines. I glide down, pulled downward.
- There is a pool of luminous intensity: amber, with blue reflexes. I get in. The pool starts rising, it rises. It envelops the body: inside and outside. It rises. It is all around. It rises to eye-level. It stops for a moment, then closes on the top.
- A line, a blue speckling goes down to the area of the will. It already distinguishes the right from the left side.
- Lines of intensity gather and spread out from the two lower areas in the peripheral vision, right and left. They gather in front of the vibratory center. They spread and extend it. I do all of this by always using the amber luminosity with blue reflexes.
- While I hold the vibratory flow, that streams forward, the mind empties itself into the flow, is driven away. It comes out of the eyes, like fog or smoke.
- The perception broadens on the time line. It moves forward, then expands without limits. The right and the left sides are pulled, put into tension by the force of perception, but do not yet separate.
- The flow from the vibratory center expands, goes toward four precise, diagonal directions: two upward and two downward, toward the four areas of peripheral vision. The extensions vibrate, have fluctuations, waves.
- These wavelike motions reverberate on the center for decisions, the upper intensification points, the right and left sides. It is as though I were breathing through my sides. Eventually, they stabilize, connecting the will and the unbending intent, like a disk or a circular flow, external but also internal.

- The circular flow enters the legs' fibers, releases details from inside the thighs, the knees, all the way to the feet. It does it using the amber luminosity with blue reflexes. It connects again to the pool of intensity and goes back up again to the connection between will and intent.
- The circular flow rises and spills over at the level of the vibratory center. It turns around as it rises, inverts its internal-external flow. From outside, from the expanded perception of before, comes a precise pressure. The circular flow gathers it by inverting direction again: external-internal. It comes back to the will and unbending intent and spreads what is obtained from the outside as it rises back up to the center for decisions. The flow turns around again, internal-external, as it goes down, settles on the line of the will, receives another impulse from the emanations outside.
- It turns again: external-internal. The whole vibratory aspect connects, extends into the diagonals, which again release vibrations.
- The vibration goes down to the ring of the will – unbending intent. It flows down the legs' back fibers, frees the details from their fibers, releases them. It goes further down, latches onto the pool of intensity, comes back up, still with the amber luminosity and the blue reflexes. It stabilizes on the unbending intent.
- At this point, I have lost my physical confines already. I am elaborating all of this in the luminous egg, in the area of possibilities.
- The unbending intent connects to the flow of the vibratory aspect, regulates and modulates it. Then it concentrates it into a core of intensity. Finally, it pushes the core of intensity to coincide, insert it into the will.

- The will extends its fibers down into the earth, to the right and left. It hooks, connects, maintains the connection in the earth, firm on both sides, right and left. The two sides are put in tension, but do not separate. Then, the will extends forward; it touches the emanations outside that respond and flow into the will's free channels until they reach it. They go down the fibers that connect us to the earth, latch on, connect to each other. The lines of the earth, the will, the emanations outside. This round trip continues until it stabilizes.
- Then it rises back into the two sides, right and left, beyond the physical confines. It reaches the vibratory center, enters the free channels of the vibratory aspect's flow, reaches the emanations outside, touches them, they respond, are inserted into the free channels; they reach and gather the vibratory aspect into a compact core that goes down and is inserted into the will.
- I work these connections out some more. I go down toward the two lower areas, in the peripheral vision, right and left. Every time I do it the right and the left sides get pulled, one with respect to the other. But, again, they do not separate.
- I connect again the unbending intent and the will, up to the emanations outside, to the areas below, right and left. The right and the left sides are pulled. But, still, they do not separate. I pass by the unbending intent, move up to the vibratory aspect that reaches the emanations outside, which respond, flow into the free channels. I come back down, to the two lower areas, to the right and left. They pull the two sides apart, but still they do not separate.
- I return to the unbending intent, go up to the intensification points and the center for decisions, and extend everything forward, up to the emanations outside; I touch them. They respond. They enter the free channels of the center for decisions

in two separate beams, connected at the intensification points: right and left. They gather on two sides, extend outwards, to the right and left, touch the emanations outside that react, latch onto, entangle my intensity fibers right and left, pull. Both sides separate.

- They separate both in front and in the back; along the whole vertical, central line of the luminous egg. I keep this opening, a special shiver rising up the back, freeing the area of perception, freeing the area of the glow… and look through the crack I have opened.
- The opening of the two sides is also above us, where a current connected to the area of the glow and the wings of perception is freed, lifted.
- The current comes back down, like a waterfall. It enters the four lateral flows, front and back, and starts going down, fine-tuning all the centers with the amber luminosity with blue reflexes.
- The four flows stabilize all the way down. The center for decisions is open, the area of the glow is expanded: they correspond.
- The wings pull to the right and left; they latch onto the emanations outside. They pull: they open the two sides even more.
- The double perception is clear. It is like having two faces turned in two different directions. To the front, where it is open, and to the right side, looking at the firm reflection of interpretation.
- I maintain the double perception as I change side: so, looking ahead, where it is open, and to the left side, along the time line. The left side opens, the right side is solid. All the directions are clear to me at the same time. The left side opens.

- The left side opens, it merges with the emanations outside. It touches them; they respond. I look into the depth of the time line, in the left side. I insert a characteristic of my perception, tied to the intimacy of the will, that touches something in the extreme distance. It is an infinite distance and, at the same time, it is close, always behind the reflection of the world.
- There is an answer that starts like a wave that flows on the surface beyond the time line, ampler. It exerts a particular pressure on my left side, a soft pressure.
- I gather myself and return to the frontal direction. Then I insert into this pressure open on the left side some lines from my centers, inserted like solid wedges, lines that govern this pressure, give it stability, definition. I secure them well to their place and use them as a fixed point to move backwards. I am outside the pressure. I see it where I was before.
- I change direction. I shift the opening of the left side toward the protected area, rotating it. I define it precisely with respect to the right side. The right side, firm, compact, borders on the area of pressure of what has been released along the time line, beyond the surface of the luminous egg.
- I shift the attention into the right side, control, observe the dynamics of the rolling force through the reflection, not directly. The right side and the left are clearly different. The right eye and the left eye are clearly different.
- I use the diagonals, constructed with the vibratory aspect, to firmly anchor myself to the earth. I extend the left side into the open part, welded to the emanations outside, obtaining different dynamics between the right and left sides. The eyes differentiate.
- The pressure that slides, grazing the right side, starts moving, flowing, passing, then returning, in a cycle that I begin recognizing.

- Every time I extend the left side further I use the difference that is created in the right side to harmonize the dynamics of the right side with that of the force in cyclical movement right outside the right side.
- When I have fully understood the correspondence of the movement, I leave, accompany, allow the dynamics of the external force to latch onto and couple in parallel with that of my right side. This also affects the left side, that does not only extend, but assumes a cyclical movement of its own that is different from the right side's but coincides in the end as beginning and end, and then again beginning, end, etc.
- The moment this coincidence occurs, I return to the direction ahead, rotating the left side again, and close the space between the two sides.
- I have included new lines, new fibers, new blue reflexes inside me. I wait for them to settle, to reach a position. Then I drag them to the vibratory aspect and extend them along the diagonal directions, toward the peripheral concentration areas, and then along the horizontal direction, broadening it.
- There is a new configuration, one with directions that are not included in the inventory. I lift and then make these extensions of the blue fibers converge toward the wings of perception, unify them; then I insert them into the four lateral flows. I let them go down the lateral flows. As they descend, rotating the lateral flows, I open and extend the time line, using these new properties.
- When the time line is completely extended, I let myself flow along it; I am like hanging, hooked. I flow. I choose a point, break loose and let myself slide into that time niche, into that time mode. I let it settle. With an impulse, a push, I get out, latch

again onto the time line, allow myself to flow, break loose, go down into another time mode.

- I get out with a push. I latch onto the time line again: still. I position myself on one of the diagonals I made before, that I made with the blue fiber and the vibratory aspect. I connect the two intensification points to this diagonal band, up to the right and down to the left, and wait for my inner configuration to be reorganized along this trajectory. The sensation is of being non-linear, asymmetric.
- This asymmetry releases intensity as dense matter, as mixed amber and blue luminosity, at the bottom of the diagonal. With the unbending intent, I move and distribute it on the right side and the power centers.
- I change diagonal, inverting the intensification points: up to the left, down to the right. The previous asymmetric configuration is exactly balanced by this new asymmetry. The nucleus of intensity is formed below to the right; I maneuver it with the unbending intent, distributing it on the left side and the power centers.
- I overlay the two previous energy configurations. I am already creating the temporary double, the one we will then find at the end. It is the energetic realization of the double perception. Two nuclei of intensity are formed down below, to the right and left; I maneuver them with the unbending intent.
- I distribute their effect upward, mixing the blue and amber fibers. The upper areas of peripheral perception, the area of the glow, the flow at the top of the skull get freed. Again, maneuvering with the unbending intent, I insert the fibers into the four lateral flows. As they go down, I open and extend the time line. The opening, the extension of the time line coincides with

the time taken by the amber and blue luminosity to go down the lateral flows.

- When it gets to the bottom of the flows, there is a coincidence along the time line, where nuclei of intensity are released to the right and left, which I maneuver with the unbending intent and make coincide and merge with the center for decisions.

- The two higher intensification points are freed; I open a vast level of intensity at their level. It coincides with the emanations outside, with infinity. Two currents respond, right and left, that go through the intensification points and flow to the vibratory center and then, fine-tuning on both sides, glide down and insert themselves into the will.

- The unbending intent gathers, recalling these two currents to its center, reuniting them into two defined and concentrated lines. Then, using this gathered essence, it governs the extension of the time line in all directions. One at a time, I find myself looking directly into the time line in four directions. In every direction, I confirm the time line at a precise distance. I do it for the right side and then for the left, in the four directions, first in a direction and then in the other. The unbending intent can now choose in what direction and how much to flow along the time line by pointing the perception directly to it.

- In this new space, wide but defined, I use the blue fibers to start releasing the dreamer's memories from the lower part of the body, make them rise and let them gather, reach an order. Then I modify it, distribute these fibers and order them into a linear configuration, open to infinity.

- I change direction, looking into the other side of the time line. I use the earth's blue fibers, mixed with the amber ones, to release the dreamer's memories from the lower part of the body. I let them gather also into this side and then change their layout: now they are ordered toward infinity.

- I bring everything to converge into and harmonize with the vibratory aspect. I spread it into the whole luminous egg, go down with my roots into the earth. The earth responds, turns the whole luminous egg on, puts the amber and the blue aspects into the right order and relationship. I repeat this passage of ordered intensity until I am certain of the consistency of the new configuration, of the balance between the amber and blue aspects. The impulse from the earth goes through, turns on, orders gently, with elegance.
- I use the boost from the earth, the last impulse, like a jolt that separates the layers of the luminous egg; lightly. It is a shock that lifts all the layers, that shows, in the double perception, the difference between fullness and the emptiness, between Tonal and Nagual. Then the layers settle again, maintaining the definition between full and empty, one layer after the other, empty-full, empty-full….
- There is no more space for useless forms. What is not consistent with the configuration obtained in this way goes out, is expelled. It is a nucleus of definition of the personal image. We seize it with the unbending intent, observe it, and disperse it in the dark sea of awareness, we let it float away.
- I use the intensification points and the wings of perception to separate the right and the left side again. They hook onto the emanations outside and separate the two sides.
- I define the four lateral flows and use them to lift the inner silence. Transparent; lucid, the amber and blue luminosity rises, purifying, cleansing the luminosity until it fills up everything. The patina of awareness shines with inner silence.

- I shift the attention into the right side, soften the patina of awareness until it is permeable to the world's silence that enters, spreads, merges with the one inside. The reflection of the description on the surface of the luminous egg does not exist anymore.
- The silence of the world rotates on the luminous egg until it is in front of me and permeates the left side, too. The two sides are separate.
- I open and extend the time line. There are no confines. The inner and outer silences coincide along the time line. I look into the time line and wait for the ability to recognize my social nucleus. I stop it in front of me, intend the sweeping breath as flow of emanations governed by the discipline that rearranges my social nucleus, adapting it to the strategic needs.
- Now I can "wear" it again. It is modified according to the coherence between the amber and blue aspects. The will governs this process, coordinating with the eyes and the intent of the sweeping breath.
- I use the coordination between the will, eyes and unbending intent to look and search in the open space between the left and right side for the coincidence with intent. The moment I seize it, I use the connection between eyes and will to drag it to the connection between the will and unbending intent.
- Every time I can drag the sensation of the presence of intent into the will, a piece of self-absorption is released. This release frees me from a tie and makes me change direction. I do the same maneuver a few more times.
- The last time, I fine-tune the will and the vibratory aspect to close the two sides. I have substituted parts of my image with quotas of intent. What I contain is different: essential, light.

- I use *seeing* to anticipate the interpretation and obtain knowledge, information. I let it arrive into the spaces that are no longer occupied by the description of myself.
- I coincide with the earth again, through the will and the vibratory aspect. I make an ample current that reaches the deepest possible layers of the earth, the innermost, the most intimate.
- I flow along this current, this channel, down to the maximum point I have reached, and then back again, quickly. When I get out and return to the starting point, I am completely emptied, cleansed, with all the luminous fibers deprived of any debris, shiny. At the same time, I use the lateral flows to open the luminous egg again and allow the entrance of intent as a conscious force that fills the free spaces.
- I let the right and left sides close naturally, go back to coincide again, to seal. I look directly into the time line, use the modulated breath to single out and select the perception of the dreamer. Now, for an instant, I coincide with myself looking at myself, with the energy body remembering.
- I do a last preparation of the energy configuration. I apply unbending intent to push, with amber and blue pressure, the right side into the left and create a void that recalls the dreamer's memories. Then I do the same thing, pushing the left side into the right.
- Next, I bring the assemblage point inward, toward the vibratory aspect, enough to make first and second attention coincide. I let it slide internally to its right positioning.
- I redefine the right and left sides. I use the permeability created by the world's silence in the luminous egg, on its surface, to issue, emanate a flow of awareness of the blue type toward my right side, removed at a certain distance. Then, I let the left side

rotate and do the same thing, making these two emanations coincide.

- I slide along the time line and coincide with this copy obtained from the blue emanations. I let them settle, recreating the balance between the amber aspect and the blue aspect.
- Thus, I look again directly into the time line and there I coincide, I am in front of the dreamer and then coincide in two positions and coincide with the dreamer, with the energy body.

ON THE CONFINES OF THE LUMINOUS EGG

It is done at a distance from the body that is much greater compared to the normal execution and with often just barely hinted movements. It is half-way between executing it physically and intending it, also because in many passages we cannot reach with our hands a distance that can involve the limits of the luminous egg.

Thus, we are forced to resort to greater abstraction.

For this reason, it is incredibly effective in attracting the energy body.

I have no way of explaining it in a book, because I decided to point out its existence, since it is very likely that, as one progresses in the knowledge of the sequence, this way of doing it will present itself spontaneously. Knowing that it exists and that it is something effective, you will also know that you are not doing it wrongly but are following new ways of understanding, devoid of explanation, free of the need to "understand."

WITH THE MOBILITY OF THE EYES TO FOLLOW THE VARIATIONS IN TIME

It is one of the most "advanced" forms of execution, as it requires at its foundation the active understanding of multiple, abstract elements: first of all, the connection eyes – will.

It is what I already mentioned in the part concerning the refinements, in: *The Discipline of Actions – Patience – The Preparation*. It is that type of softness and movement in the double perception.

The key point is being able to associate the eyes to the internal continuity flows, using the double perception. Then our eyes will acquire a very peculiar type of movement: a movement that, in a mysterious way, is done by the whole body; that we perceive as being done by the whole body.

Yet, it is not associated to physical movements in any way. There is a reason: the continuity flows are the fullness to which we latch our perception; the continuity gaps are the emptiness in which we physically move. They are the two faces of the same coin, the positive and negative in a film. They are the same thing, but in the opposite space.

Therefore, the eyes follow the trajectories of the variations in the energy configuration, reflected on the emanations outside; in other words, they follow the variation of the alignment that ensues from the shift of the assemblage point position.

IN DREAMING

Once the sequence is fully assimilated, that is, when our body executes it without any mental intervention, we can try reproducing it in the lucid dreams that we might have.

This type of execution has a very special effect on our dreaming, or better, on the dreaming position we have reached. It makes it immediately stabler; the dreaming takes on uniformity and cohesion. It becomes consistent, extremely "real."

This effect is due both to the action of the movements on the maneuverability and stability of the assemblage point and to the fact of having a very precise purpose for dreaming.

Then, there are other remarkable effects.

Every single movement in the sequence has a specific intent that, in dreaming, is activated in a very clear way. We will find this advantage later on, when we perform the sequence awake.

Moreover, every movement can lead to the dreaming position consequent to its intent.

In dreaming we can also "see" the way the energy is manipulated by the different movements.

The sequence, furthermore, is endowed with an unavoidable intent: the predominance of the energy body. In dreaming, it becomes incredibly more accessible. The dreamer is already there, a step away. The way the sequence leads to the energy body in dreaming allows us to disengage our dreaming from the fetters that we could drag into it along with ourselves.

We do the sequence in dreaming and, from the moment in which, eventually, we coincide with the dreamer, it recovers possession of its entire abilities.

There is another effect that has immense interest for dreaming: the sequence leads to the blue worlds by using the right fractions of inorganic energy.

To help yourself obtain the guide to the blue worlds, use the mobility of the eyes as described above.

MAKING THE TRANSITION

This one cannot be even considered as a special form: it is what should happen, sooner or later, as one practices the sequence.

It is an open door on stalking and controlled folly.

The stalker's dream is accessed by making the transition in the course of an action and by fulfilling it effectively. The most evolved case is the one in which, to make the transition, we use a social node of ours in the course of a social interaction.

What does “making the transition” mean? From the point of view of the subjective experience, it means falling asleep while staying awake. From the point of view of the seers, it means moving the assemblage point intentionally, maintaining the heightened awareness active; or, also, modifying the time mode deliberately, without losing the ability to act and interact.

It is what must take place during the sequence; the moment of the sequence when it happens depends on our level of silence, energy, and attention. But it is what must, sooner or later, occur.

INTENDED WHILE MAKING THE TRANSITION

We can intend the sequence while falling asleep (even lying in bed), making the transition and entering dreaming directly.

We must enter and continue the sequence in dreaming all the way to the end. This stabilizes the dream and leads to the predominance of the energy body, giving us immediately our skills as dreamers.

An ideal moment to make the transition is during “*The Effect of Silence.*”

The series of boosts we obtain allows us to overcome the membrane, the confines to the other world, much more easily.

SYNCHRONOUS WITH OTHER ELEMENTS OF THE WORLD

It is possible to do the sequence synchronically with other elements of the world; for instance, with a tree or a group of trees, even with a whole woods or any other kind of natural element.

What makes it possible is the sequence's characteristic of harmonizing the reciprocal interference of the energy fibers that make up the involved beings.

The more precise is our perceptual sensitivity connected to the movements, the easier it is to establish a pragmatic, active relationship with the element of the world with which we are becoming synchronized.

The purposes of this type of execution are quite varied and also depend on the imagination skills, on the fluidity and availability of a warrior.

We can facilitate the parallel movement with the chosen element, establish an agreement to find it in our dreaming, acquire specific potential, or make many other things. Obviously, what counts is to be able to use the sequence in order to intend what we decide to intend.

A very special application of this way of doing the sequence is to execute it in the places of coincidence (or "power" places). Clearly, the first requirement in this case is the ability to recognize a place of coincidence and its characteristics; otherwise, it is not possible to direct the intent of the sequence to make it synchronic with the place itself.

If one can do it, also in this case, the possibilities are many. We can make the place energetically "practicable", orient its characteristics, acquire its potential, access new assemblage point positions.

Regardless of the ability to recognize the place, the sequence acts all the same so as to “tame” the places in which it is performed.

WITH MIRRORS

I add this possibility only to make you aware of its existence. Describing it in this setting is impossible; it requires first of all the understanding of the discipline of mirrors and then the transposition of the sequence into this discipline. It is something I show during the practical retreats; it can only be transmitted directly.

Thus, this mention is mainly for the benefit of those who already know the use of mirrors. The sequence can be done with two 7x14 inches mirrors, used to enhance the effect of the sequence on the layers of energy fibers. The result is really disruptive, both on the perceptual state and on the intensity of our awareness.

The movements are a great deal more fluid, compared to when we practice it without the mirrors, because the mirrors continuously latch onto our fibers and pull them, creating an elastic effect that reverberates on the physical movements.

CREATING AND SUSTAINING A PLACE OF COINCIDENCE

We can exploit the force with which the principle underlying the reiteration channels and consolidates the attention, to create a "personal place of coincidence."

As I was saying above, the sequence tends to orient the characteristics of a place, to "tame" it. If we add the force of the reiteration to this, we can really obtain a very special place for us.

First of all, we have to start with a place whose traits are favorable to us, if nothing else, to avoid making our job too difficult and long. Let us choose a place where we will do the sequence and do it there almost every day, in order to modify its configuration. It really becomes a personal place of coincidence.

However, make sure you carry out the action in the right manner, otherwise it will be only partially effective.

Therefore, respect the reiteration principles. Always go to the same exact point, orientated toward the same direction, look at the same points, etcetera.

This means that you will need the first times to decide well how to orientate yourself, where to start, how to use your eyes.

You will realize, when it starts working, that the purpose of this execution mode is not limited to creating a place of coincidence; or better, that, as the place starts interacting with you, other very interesting things happen.

For instance, the sequence will "execute itself," the body will move independently, precisely because of the interaction with the place.

The sensations will arrive spontaneously and will be a great deal clearer, more defined.

You will access with greater ease the double perception.
You will understand the nature of the internal continuity flows and continuity gaps.
And a lot more….

THE VARIATION FOR THE TONAL

When I am at the "*Lines of Force,*" my hands do not go down along the lateral flows, but I go directly to "*Opening the Time Line.*"
So I skip the whole part that opens the left side and puts us in relationship with the rolling force.
Executing the sequence in this way deeply modifies its effect. It leads the power of the predominance of the energy body to shift toward stalking, toward the strategic actions in the tonal, toward the integration of magical attitudes into the first attention.
It is very useful when facing practical matters.

EXECUTION IN PARALLEL

In order for you to understand this type of execution in depth, it can be helpful for me to tell you how my teachers have transmitted the sequence to me, because their teaching method was precisely based on the execution in parallel.

This tale will make what the sequence really is a lot clearer.

The house where I used to meet with my teachers, in Central Mexico, had a very special room. They defined it as "the territory of unbending intent."

You could access this environment by a very strange route through the house, until you arrived in an octagonal, underground room with a roof on wooden beams.

The environment had no windows, only narrow splits similar to embrasures, whose opening could be adjusted. This allowed to obtain more or less intense blades of light, that could be dimmed to complete darkness.

Furthermore, a part of the roof was equipped with a moving section that allowed to open a passage to a view of the sky, with daylight or at night.

What characterized the room, though, was the presence of a very particular bed, a "nest."

The latter consisted in a solid frame suspended up high, at the center of the room, right under the mobile section of the roof, through cables secured to the beams of the roof. The frame itself contained a very strong cloth equipped with rings along the hemline in which various ropes passed, tying the cloth to the frame. Both the tension of the cables and of the ropes were adjustable, thus obtaining a whole range of levels of stability, flotation, and overall positioning of the structure.

Furthermore, there was a whole set of cables in the room, at a certain height, placed in such a way as to allow to position other special "nests" along the walls or at the corners of the room.

These were made of the same strong cloth as the central bed and were equipped with rings with snap-hooks along the hemlines, so that they could be hung up on the cables.

Once installed, they allowed a person to get inside the nest in the dreamer's position, that is, with the soles of the feet united, legs spread and adhering to the cloth that enveloped the person; or in other postures, depending on the case.

The purposes of the room and the bed were various and depended on attitudes that were developed from time to time. On one side, they were based on the ability of the overall structure to favor the mobility of the assemblage point; on the other side, on the fact that being suspended in that way allowed to part more easily from one's convictions and contradictions.

My teachers used that environment many times to pursue the most varied goals; maneuvers relevant to dreaming, stalking, the relationship with intent, or the possibilities provided by the mastery of awareness.

In the case of the sequence, that was the place in which they transmitted it to me as a series of assemblage point movements.

Their teaching technique in this respect was very different from what can be imagined; the sequence was taught to me in the opposite way a series of movements is usually transmitted. I was a real not-doing.

The assemblage point has the characteristic trait of latching onto and following the movements and positions that are energetically most efficient, if one is willing to do it and does not oppose it.

The seers in my lineage have been exploiting this trait for generations, implementing what they call the "movement in parallel;" and they do it to prove to their apprentices the existence and maneuverability of the assemblage point.

In short, what they did was, first of all, using that room to induce me to follow the shifts of the assemblage point that they did as they were intending the sequence. Note that I said "intending the sequence."

We would meet in there; I lay in the suspended structure in order to perceive the movement and positioning of the assemblage point with the greatest possible exactness. They positioned themselves in the nests all around the room and started intending the sequence in unison. I had to reach inner silence, open the left side, and let their intending maneuver my assemblage point.

We did it numberless times, to permit my body to register a series of positions and movements.

The next step they asked my to carry out was to realize precisely what physical sensations and changes in perception and state of awareness were associated with the assemblage point movements.

On the basis of these "samples of sensations," they finally guided me to recognize them and associate the correct physical movements and the use of the eyes and attention that could recall those same sensations that, in turn, produce the shifts of the assemblage point.

This whole process required a lot of time and commitment, but they did it in order to endow me with the ability to develop the sequence beyond its most superficial and evident aspects.

Thus, I was able to connect the sequence to its intent, predetermined by generations of warriors, and to the flow of the infinite sea of awareness.

In this way, it can live of its own life and continue guiding me and the people who will learn it to the possibility of opening further passages into the unknown.

Obviously, the way I teach the sequence cannot reproduce theirs. However, it is possible to learn to perform it in parallel, pursuing the opposite path I followed; thus, starting from the first attention.

In this case, this is the procedure: learning the physical movements, associating the right sensations, singling out the shifts and assemblage point positions.

So, the sequence becomes a way of realizing about the existence of the assemblage point and its maneuverability. It is a very safe way, which provides the right inner strength and discipline.

I will suggest a few ways to do it, which I already use in my retreats.

To begin, it is obviously necessary to have one or more people who have correctly learned the sequence, at least as far as the movements and the main line of the sensations associated to the movements are concerned. Further refinement can ensue from the parallel execution on the part of the people who do not do the movements directly but follow them only perceptively.

Two main methods are possible. In both cases, there will be one or more persons who perform the sequence physically and others who "follow it from a still point."

In the first, the people standing still, positioned around those who do it physically, simply watch and allow their assemblage point to be pulled. This translates into sensations or perceptual states that are more or less marked.

I advise not to watch the movements directly when people do the sequence, but to keep them in the area of the peripheral vision. In this way, it is a lot easier to move on the sensations, excluding the tendency of mental commenting and personal judgment.

With the other method, those who follow standing still must be isolated sensorially.

They must be in the same environment, which can be either inside or outside.

The persons who do the sequence and those who follow it mix uniformly in the environment. The latter, however, must not be able to see those who execute it; instead, they must be put in conditions that favor the fluidity of the assemblage point. Ideally, they should be inside recapitulation tents or suspended on shamanic nests. From this privileged position, they stop the inner dialogue and latch onto the execution of the sequence. It is a condition in which it is possible to get to the precise perception of the assemblage point shift and thus allow the assemblage point to be pulled along the correct track.

In both cases, those who stay still and follow should then record their sensations and perceptions with the highest possible exactness, so as to further refine the general execution.

The sequence is pure intent

THE VIDEO

In order to learn the movements of the Sequence correctly, the book goes with a video that shows its execution.

Initially, the video was in a DVD attached to the book; however, I have later decided to separate them, uploading the video on the Internet. Presently, you can find it on the website (www.nagualism.org) and on YouTube channel.

It is essential that you follow the video during the learning phase.

The video is studied so as to allow you to follow the sequence the way it is divided in the book, movement by movement.

Enjoy your learning experience.